Lincoln Highway 101

John Mulhern III

SECOND EDITION

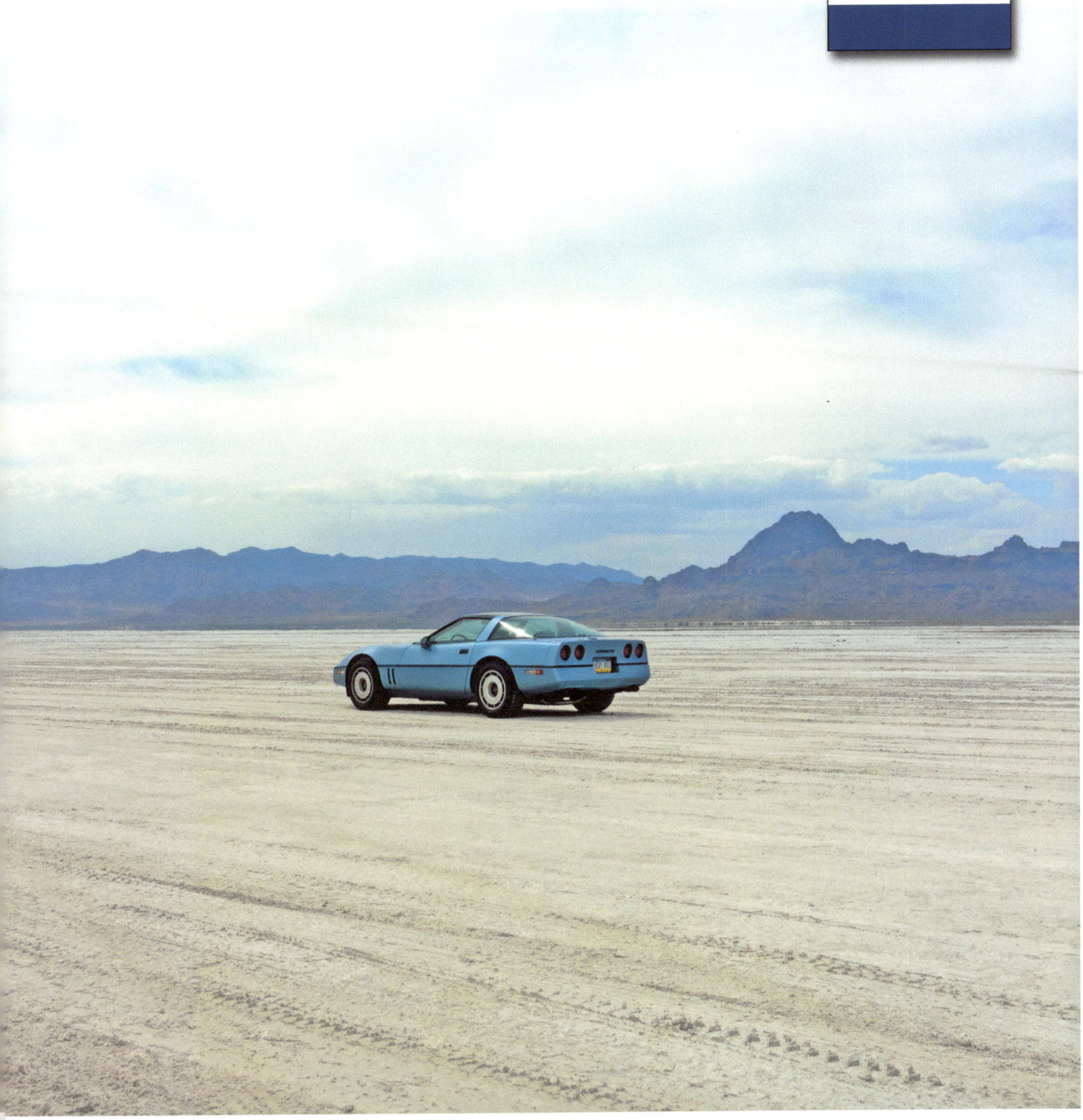

Copyright © 2018 by J3Studio Press
ISBN 978-0-9971674-0-5
All rights reserved.
This book may not be reproduced, in whole or in part, including illustrations, in any form (beyond that copying permitted by Sections 107 and 108 of U.S. Copyright Law and except by reviewers for the public press), without written permission from the author.

Edited by Vern Yoneyama

Designed by John Mulhern III
Set in Adobe Caslon Pro, Copperplate Gothic, Lato, and Myriad Pro type by John Mulhern III

Front cover: Ivelis waits patiently inside *Lauren* outside the Nebraska's Lincoln Highway Visitors Center in Shelton, Nebraska
Page i: *Lauren* on the Bonneville Salt Flats in western Utah
Back cover: *Lauren* at the roadside park in Tama, Iowa

To my glorious wife Ivelis, without whom even consideration of this trip or this book would have been impossible

In memory of my paternal grandfather, Lieutenant Colonel John Mulhern, who influenced me far more than I think he knew

Table of Contents

Author's Notes — IV
A Few Reasons Why I Wrote This Book • A Second Edition of a Self-Published Book?
Acknowledgments and Thanks • About the Maps

Prologue — IX
A Short History of the Lincoln Highway • Where My Love of Cars Comes From
An All-New Corvette Makes an Impression • A Similar Color on Another Relevant Car

History and Preparation — XI
Another Corvette Comes First • Searching for Light Blue Metallic • Finally Finding *Lauren*
What a 1985 Corvette Is • That Improved and Cool-Looking Engine
1985 Corvette Equipment and Costs • Perhaps the Real Reason We Took This Trip
Some Non-Trivial Vehicle Preparation • There Must Be Appropriate Music!
Planning for the Trip Itself • Our Specific Lincoln Highway Route
Significant Concerns Remain

Staging to Manhattan: Bryn Mawr, Pennsylvania to New York City, New York — 1
Heading for the Eastern Terminus • One of the Greatest Hotels in the World
Checking off a Longtime Dining Goal

The Way Out, Part I: New York City, New York to Warsaw, Indiana — 3
And Here We Go! • Our First Diner of the Trip • A Quick Stop Back Home
Not Going Exactly According to Plan • Lovely and Historic Gettysburg
Two Points of Attraction in a Tiny Town • Our Second Stay in Pittsburgh
Day Two on the Lincoln Highway • The Old Route Makes Its Presence Felt
A Late but Really Great Lunch at Kewpee • "Seedling Miles"

The Way Out, Part II: Warsaw, Indiana to North Platte, Nebraska — 15
Country Driving in Northwestern Indiana • Traveling Due West Just South of Chicago
Visiting Franklin Grove • The Old Highway Reveals Itself
Stopping for a Distinctive Bridge in Tama • Some Quite Frightening Weather
Returning to Normal? • Trains, Trains, and Yet More Trains • Some Positive and Negative Stops
Two Classic American Tourist Traps

The Way Out, Part III: North Platte, Nebraska to West Wendover, Nevada — 27
Departing for Rock Springs • Long Closed, but Yet Still Hanging Around
Unexpected Equipment Failure • Details, Details, Details • Visiting the Luxury Diner
"Somewhere West of Laramie" • Rain in Dry Wyoming • Toward a Potential Technology Fix
Downtown in Salt Lake City • Returning to the Highway
One Item Removed From a Bucket List

The Way Out, Part IV: West Wendover, Nevada to San Francisco, California — 39
Early Morning in Northeastern Nevada • Absolute Carnage in Ely, Nevada
Finding Help at Precision Auto Repair • A Relaxed Breakfast Helps Decompress
"The Loneliest Road in America" • An Entertaining Night in Stateline
Our Excellent Camera Goes Missing • Serious Problems in California Traffic • The Big Finish
The First Real Hotel Since Pittsburgh

The Way Back, Part I: San Francisco, California to Denver, Colorado   49
  Starting Back East *Really Quickly* • A Relaxing Visit with Bill • Back on the Road
  Lauren Makes It to 75,000 Miles • One Final Bonus on Memorial Day
  The Right Roads for *Lauren* • Entering Colorado From the West
  Down Some Horsepower at Altitude • Denver, Always Wonderful

The Way Back, Part II: Denver, Colorado to Indianapolis, Indiana   55
  Leaving Denver Fairly Slowly • There Are Clearly Other Cool Cars
  Downtown Kansas City Astonishes • Heading Toward Indy • Searching for a Sonic
  Impressive Indianapolis

The Way Back, Part III: Indianapolis, Indiana to Bryn Mawr, Pennsylvania   61
  The First of Two Great Museums • Another Amazing Museum • Walking in Columbus
  One Final Day on the Road • A Brand New Corvette Motivates

Afterword   65
  A Few Conclusions • Some of What's Happened Since the Trip

Lists   67
  Cassette Tapes in the Center Console • Equipment and Tools in the Car
  Our Bests of the Trip • Things That I Know We Missed

Annotated Bibliography   69

Index   71

Credits   75

One photograph neatly encompasses the essence of the Lincoln Highway experience; markers, trains, and restoration near Overton, Nebraska

Author's Notes

A Few Reasons Why I Wrote This Book
I wrote this book in part because I wanted to have an account of how interesting and different it was to travel in the mid-2010s in *Lauren*, my beloved but sometimes trying 1985 Chevrolet Corvette coupe.

I also wrote this book because many folks that we know in the car hobby assumed that I would—I think mostly because of a book (*A 21st Century Road Trip*) I wrote back in 2006 about a journey along Route 66 and the Pacific Coast Highway in a far newer Corvette.

Finally, I wanted to tell the story of our trip in May 2014, both because I thought that other people might find it engaging and sometimes (often?) amusing and because I didn't want to let any of the details of this particular trip fade away over time.

I wanted this book to work both for Corvette enthusiasts and for people who know nothing or next to nothing about Corvettes or other collector cars. So, there are explanations of some Corvette things that many Corvette people may find more than a bit elementary and that some non-Corvette people may judge as far too extensive. I hope the reader will forgive this inability to leave any supposedly needed explanation out.

A Second Edition of a Self-Published Book?
A second edition seems at least somewhat pretentious in a self-published book, but I felt that I needed to make another run at this particular story. After I had completed another Corvette-centric travel book (*Slightly Slower 66*) in late 2015, it became painfully apparent to me that I had missed many opportunities for optimization in the first edition of this book—at least somewhat because it had been so long (eight years) since I had published *any* book.

In raw numbers, this second edition has 14 more pages than the first version and over 13,800 additional words (about 67% more). There are also over 65 added images with every one of the photographs included having significantly better color correction. Finally, there are *vastly* improved and far more detailed maps—there are now 27 of the particular Lincoln Highway route taken where there were previously only four. More importantly than the numerically measured increases, I believe this version of the book is notably more coherent and leaves far less out.

135-year-old Eureka Opera House stands proud in small (population 610) Eureka, Nevada

Acknowledgments and Thanks
First, thanks to my wife Ivelis, for her assistance, support, understanding, and most of all, her great love.

Thanks to Vern Yoneyama, who made *many* substantial attempts at editing this much-revised second edition. Any slip-ups that missed his eagle eye are mine alone.

If the typography in this book is anything resembling acceptable, it is chiefly due to what I have learned from Nigel French, of lynda.com and elsewhere.

Thanks to Margaret Antkowiak, Rob Corder, Allyson Fredeen, Bill Hetzel, Kylee Markey, Jordan McClead, Caecilia Mulhern, Debra Schrampfer, and Adam Wald for assistance in securing the rights to images and photographs. Thanks once again to Margaret Antkowiak for family-related fact checking. Thanks to Larry Teufel and Jim Swart for fact-checking related to *Lauren*'s very early years in Portland. Thanks to Mark Frankel for Eighties

Chevrolet-related context and fact-checking—it was also great to reconnect with Mark after all those years. Thanks also to Michael Heath for photographic equipment advice, to Celeste Stewart for general authoring advice, and to Kevin O'Connor for *very* patient color correction assistance.

Thanks to the Lincoln Highway Association for their enthusiastically given information and useful context.

The people who worked with me to bring *Lauren* up to her impressive condition as of mid-2014 were many; the ones who come quickly to mind are, in alphabetical order, Greg Cue, Dave Perry, John Porter, and (last but certainly not least) Bob Zimmerman. Jim Stuempfle and Justin Luton from County Corvette in West Chester, PA have also been very helpful over the previous 12 years—even back when the idea of actually restoring a mid-1980s Corvette was a somewhat strange one.

Contemporary Corvette, a late-model Corvette-specific junkyard (!) in Bristol, PA, was especially valuable back when I was first beginning to restore *Lauren*. Far more locally (within two miles of our house), Armen Chevrolet and United Tire & Service of Rosemont both have been of considerable help.

Thanks to the folks on the Corvette Guru and the Corvette Forum websites for information, fact-checking, and (patient) assistance both before and after the trip.

Finally, thanks to Stevie Nicks for "Sable on Blond," the inspirational song for this book (even if that album track from *The Wild Heart* does predate *Lauren* by a couple of years). Listening to Stevie *rip* into the second bridge of the song, well, that's a unique Eighties experience …

About the Maps

Fairly early on in the development of this second edition, I realized that decent and reasonably detailed maps would help considerably with telling the story. All 27 maps of the Lincoln Highway portion of the trip are to the same scale—approximately an inch for every 19 miles—and that's why they vary in display size.

Various icons on those Lincoln Highway maps indicate places we stayed, where we ate and fueled, issues and fixes, and (of course) where we took photos.

Hotel marks when we stayed in a "real" full-service hotel, which happened only three times on the Lincoln Highway portion of this trip.

Motel marks the rest of our stops for the night—the reliable and moderately priced national chain motels (Best Western, Hampton Inn, Holiday Inn, etc.) that are likely to be present in any town of reasonable size.

Coffee marks when we stopped only for coffee or perhaps coffee and a light snack—and we stopped many times for coffee on this trip.

Diner marks when we stopped at one of America's greatest contributions to road food—the high value and often regionally distinctive diner. New Jersey, Pennsylvania, Wyoming (twice), and California (once on the way in and once on the way out) all provided their varying interpretations of what a diner should be to us on this trip.

Fast Food marks stops were often in the middle of the day—and often at the remarkably consistent national chains that everyone knows.

Dining marks a dining establishment both a step up from fast food but also not a diner. A few times along the route this was actual fine dining.

Fuel marks (natch!) where we stopped to fill *Lauren*'s quite capacious 20-gallon gas tank to the top—our preference on this trip was for Chevron, ExxonMobil, Phillips 66, and Sinclair gas stations.

Issue marks a new challenge of some sort—some of them easily solved, but some significantly more problematic.

Fix marks the solving, the repair, or at least the practical management of one of our existing issues, either one with the car or something else.

Photo marks where the book includes at least one photograph taken at that location, almost all of them taken with our Sony Cyber-Shot DSC-RX100, Ivelis' iPhone 4s, or my iPhone 5.

Prologue

A period map of the original 1914 Lincoln Highway route

A Short History of the Lincoln Highway

The Lincoln Highway was conceived at some point in 1912 by entrepreneur and promotional genius Carl Graham Fisher of Indiana and formally dedicated on the last day of October 1913. It ran from Times Square in New York City west to Lincoln Park in San Francisco, initially through the states of New York, New Jersey, Pennsylvania, Ohio, Indiana (no surprise!), Illinois, Iowa, Nebraska, Colorado, Wyoming, Utah, Nevada, and California—almost 3,400 miles.

The strange politically influenced loop through Colorado was removed in 1915, and a relatively late realignment relocated the Lincoln Highway through the extreme northern tip of West Virginia in 1927. Thus, there are 14 states, 128 counties, and over 700 municipalities through which the roadway passed at some time during its operating history.

In 1919, the United States Army sent 79 cars and trucks and 297 men on a trip along almost the entire Lincoln Highway—3,310 miles (the route had already shortened a bit) in 62 days making for an average speed of just over six miles per hour. An impressive medal with a small Lincoln Highway emblem nicely integrated into the ribbon portion was authorized by the War Department (we were a more blunt country a century ago) for every officer and enlisted man who completed the trip. Notably, one of the observing officers on that trip was a 28-year-old lieutenant colonel named Dwight D. Eisenhower.

Where My Love of Cars Comes From

Another lieutenant colonel from the army is also part of this story. My grandfather on my father's side (John Mulhern, Senior) was a car person, and I've known this for as long as I can remember. After bringing it through a substantial restoration, he kept a lovely red (of course!) 1963 Alfa Romeo Giulia 1600 Sprint coupe in his garage in central New Jersey for many years. In the late 1970s and early 1980s, he would mail me his copies of *Car and Driver* magazine after he had finished reading them. This thoughtful act was of notable worth to a middle-school-aged boy in those pre-Internet years.

My grandfather posing with his gorgeous Alfa Romeo Giulia 1600 Sprint

This love of automobiles almost entirely skipped my father (who was the middle of my paternal grandparent's three children) though he does admit to being a fan of nearly all Morgans and many Jaguars. However, it did not pass over his younger brother in any way. After a youth which I'm told was filled with drag-racing, my Uncle Peter worked in the automotive industry for much of his adult life, spending time with Fiat, Bertone, and Yugo. That final position led to a May 1999 mention on the front page of *The Wall Street Journal* in an article about three men who drag-raced Yugos with some success.

> "WIN A 1983 CORVETTE"
> ONLY 900 Tickets $30 each Partial proceeds benefits Children's Hospital, draw'g date May 1st at Frankel Chevrolet Ardmore. Make checks payable to: County Corvette Assoc PO Box 724B, Media Pa 19063

Chevrolet dealers had hoped against hope that there would actually be a 1983 Corvette—here's a raffle from the dealer I worked for

An All-New Corvette Makes an Impression

The first fourth-generation (C4) Corvette I saw in person had a *Light Blue Metallic* exterior. When I was a high school student in the early to mid-1980s, I worked part-time at Frankel Chevrolet (a dealership on the Lincoln Highway in Ardmore, Pennsylvania). I'll *never* forget seeing that car in early 1983, small block V8 engine with "Cross-Fire Injection" rumbling, lovely over-engineered retractable headlamps up and on, fancy new metallic paint with clear coat looking its best in the setting sun. Viewing this new vehicle was a visceral experience for a fifteen-year-old. It was the *exact* moment where my opinion of new Corvettes changed from a sort of grudging respect (I was more of a BMW and Pontiac fan at that point) to "I will have one of those someday."

Chevrolet believed *Light Blue Metallic* would be a popular color—introduction articles for the fourth-generation Corvette from *Car and Driver* and *Motor Trend*, along with a dealer promo model

In addition, when this generation of the Corvette was new, many of the Corvettes displayed on the covers of the automotive magazines of the day such as *Car and Driver* and *Motor Trend* were *Light Blue Metallic*—Chevrolet press relations evidently believed that the new Corvette was extremely attractive in that color. This belief, of course, made those publishers violate the oft-quoted canard that the best way to increase newsstand sales of an automotive magazine is to put a *red* Corvette on the cover.

A Similar Color on Another Relevant Car

Familiar and comfortable with things Japanese at least partially from his time serving in the occupation forces following World War II, my grandfather purchased a couple of first Datsun and then Nissan Maximas over the years. When Nissan announced the new and *much* sportier third-generation version of the Maxima for the 1989 model year, I (firmly convinced of my twenty-year-old hipness) assumed that he would not purchase one. I was wrong: within a year, my grandfather was driving one of those new Maximas with the "4DSC" logo (an abbreviation for "4-Door Sports Car") on a side window—an at least somewhat instructive lesson for this young man.

There is one final salient detail on that new Maxima my grandfather had acquired. It had a *Winter Blue Metallic* exterior—a color not *at all* far from *Light Blue Metallic*.

My grandfather passed away in early 1996, and many members of our large family seemed to agree that I should inherit a few of the toy cars that he had collected. I still have them, of course—they are stored carefully, but are also available for play to the much younger generation just as he made them accessible to me.

One of my greatest regrets remains that my grandfather never got to see me with any of our Corvettes. I'm sure he sensed that I would get into automobiles in a relatively significant way, given even half a chance. I'd like to think that he is looking down on Ivelis and me and our many "Big Trips" with vast amusement.

History and Preparation

Another Corvette Comes First

In late April 2003, Ivelis and I purchased a 2003 50th Anniversary Corvette convertible and took delivery at the National Corvette Museum in Bowling Green, Kentucky. Less than three months later, we were enthusiastic participants in Chevrolet's amazing 50th Anniversary Corvette Caravan and Celebration. At what Ivelis called (and still calls) "Corvette Heaven" at the Nashville Coliseum, there was a representative car for every year of Corvette production—and either the 1984 or 1985 display car was (of course) the *Light Blue Metallic* hue I discussed in this book's prologue. It reminded me of how much I liked that particular color on those early C4 model years.

It turned out that owning a Corvette was an unexpectedly involving and immersing experience—the two of us had (honestly!) thought we were merely buying a very nice new sports car. Over the next few months, we made quite a few new friends and participated frequently and enthusiastically in various cruises and other events.

Interestingly, Ivelis and I had been married for several years before we found out that we shared a specific interest in Corvettes (the two of us had known that we both liked cars in general). One evening in September 2003, Ivelis asked me over one of those great dinners she cooks about why I admired Corvettes so much. I told her the story of that 1984 Corvette arriving at the dealership in Ardmore, Pennsylvania. My lovely wife looked suddenly and very earnestly at me across the small table in our dining nook and asked an unexpected question; "How much would one of those cars cost?"

I was floored by this query—completely unprepared (and I pride myself on being ready for any question). Over the following week, I did a good bit of research and discovered that an honest but not perfect example would probably go for from between $7,500 and $12,500. When I informed Ivelis of this, she said, "If you find one, buy it." I, of course, was floored once again—but I'm a good husband, and I did what I was told.

A few years later, Ivelis told me in passing that she didn't want me to miss a chance at buying a significant car from my youth before it became too expensive for what it could reasonably return in enjoyment. This buying opportunity is a window she believes she missed with a Corvette model that she loves; the third-generation "shark" Corvette convertibles made from 1968 to 1975.

Searching for Light Blue Metallic

I believe that you should always purchase an older Corvette (or any "collectible" car for that matter) while having at least some idea of what your intentions are for it—it isn't at all the same as buying a "regular" new or used car. My central plans for the vehicle were two:

1) Enjoy driving it—Corvettes are for driving!
2) Restore it to as original as possible

Corvette colors often do come quite close to repeating; *Lauren* and I "social climbing" with Nancy and Frank Paschal and their gorgeous Silver Blue 1958 at a judged show in New Hope, Pennsylvania in August 2012

Finding a suitable *Light Blue Metallic* car turned out to be hilariously (for Ivelis) and painfully (for me) non-trivial. My quick and dirty research quickly showed that *Light Blue Metallic* was a remarkably unsuccessful color; only 2.3% of the substantial first-year production in 1984 and just 2.6% of the much lower production total in 1985—in both years the least chosen color option. Chevrolet often aggressively phases out Corvette colors that don't sell, so *Light Blue Metallic* was removed from the options list for the 1986 model year (along with two other slow-selling colors).

After some consideration, I decided that I would look for a 1985. The most significant reasons for this choice were the general additional refinements and the improved engine (we'll talk about this soon) over the 1984. With a mere 1,021 *Light Blue Metallic* cars built in 1985, NHTSA's vehicle survivability statistics told me that I could reasonably expect that only about 120 vehicles of that color would still be on the road. Of course, only a small percentage of those cars would be for sale.

Substantially complicating my search was the fact that *Light Blue Metallic* wasn't the only blue available for the 1985 model year. Chevrolet also offered a *Medium Blue Metallic* and a *Light Blue Metallic/Medium Blue Metallic* two-tone option—and both (of course) ended up being significantly more popular than *Light Blue Metallic*. In addition, many 1985 Corvettes for sale were listed only as "blue" and pictures that were taken back in late 2003/early 2004 were often not the best. These constraints meant that I spent a lot of time trying to get used car dealers and private owners to tell me which *particular* color of blue the car they were selling was. I also quickly learned to ask for a picture of the Service Parts Identification label (SPID), which showed the all-important *20L* color code (and nothing else) when it was a color I was seeking.

Finally Finding *Lauren*

After a five-month search, Ivelis and I found and bought *Lauren* over the internet from Delon BMW (!) in Salem, Oregon in February 2004. We purchased her sight unseen—but with the essential help of a certified appraisal service (I'm not *entirely* crazy).

After the transaction with Delon BMW was complete, we had *Lauren* shipped east across the United States on an open auto transporter. She arrived in eastern Pennsylvania filthy but otherwise unscathed from her (at a minimum) 2,900-mile trip. I took some quick photos as the truck driver unloaded her by the side of the interstate before carefully driving a final ten fraught miles back to our house. I had forgotten to bring any cleaning supplies, and I didn't even remember (it had been almost twenty years since I had driven a C4) how to turn the headlights on—the helpful transporter driver ended up showing me. He probably wondered at least a little about whether I knew what I was getting myself into.

A very dirty *Lauren* coming off the transporter in Plymouth Meeting, Pennsylvania in March 2004

After doing a lot of cleaning and getting at least somewhat of a handle on what the various issues with the car were, I started restoring *Lauren* in earnest in the summer of 2004, shortly after having her judged by the National Corvette Restorers Society (NCRS) for the first time. Restoration of an early C4 Corvette was and is undoubtedly an iterative process, but every six months I could look back on at least a few distinct improvements and my scores in judging confirmed this impression.

There's at least one more thing I believe you might be wondering at this point—where does that given name come from? *Lauren* was named about six months after we had purchased her and she was named (I don't remember exactly why even though I did the naming) after the lovely Lauren Hutton—*unquestionably* a classy 1980s model.

Lauren at her pre-Lincoln Highway peak, after a successful (and non-trivial) NCRS Performance Verification in Wildwood, New Jersey in June 2011

What a 1985 Corvette Is

Many people in the car hobby think of the almost all new fourth generation Corvettes as the first "modern" versions of Chevrolet's sports car, though modern is certainly a fluid concept now—more than thirty years later. Developed in the late 1970s and early 1980s, the C4s were the first Corvettes to have rack-and-pinion steering (from the 1984 model year on) and a removable one piece "targa" roof (also from 1984). They also featured futuristic-looking colored LCD gauges (from 1984 and much criticized at the time), and electronic port fuel injection (from 1985).

C4s after 1985 were also the first Corvettes with anti-lock brakes (from 1986), a six-speed manual transmission (from 1989), a selective ride and handling system (also from 1989), traction control (from 1992), and dual airbags (from 1994). Because of General Motors' substantial financial difficulties in the early 1990s, Chevrolet didn't bring another Corvette generation to market until the 1997 model year—and thirteen years is forever in the highly competitive sports car business.

Thus, *Lauren* is an early C4, and there are a lot of amazingly primitive things about her. For example, trouble codes are read with an appropriately bent paper clip inserted into the ODB-1 diagnostic port (no fancy code-readers needed here!), and one of the more critical electronic adjustments for the engine is performed with (aaack!) a mallet.

One of the salient characteristics of early C4s—especially ones with the extra cost ($470) *Z51* performance handling package, which, of course, *Lauren* has—is that they have an especially hard ride, one that edges well toward brutal. A well-known and somewhat bitter Corvette joke of the age was that, if you drove over a U.S. coin in an early C4 with the *Z51* option, you could tell whether it was a penny, nickel, dime, or quarter. The return for this discomfort was fantastic handling for the day—as long as the road was near-perfect. Along with snazzy (and very capable) Delco/Bilstein gas-charged shock absorbers, heavy duty springs, thicker stabilizer bars, quicker steering, and one-inch wider wheels, checking off the *Z51* option also got a 1985 Corvette's proud new owner an engine oil cooler and an extra radiator fan.

That Improved and Cool-Looking Engine

Since the Corvette was all new except for the engine and the automatic transmission for 1984, it was not surprising at all that the big news for the 1985 model year was a new version of Chevrolet's classic 350 cubic inch/5.7 liter "small block" V8. This engine dates from 1967, and its basic design extends all the way back to Chevrolet chief engineer Ed Cole's substantially smaller "Turbo-Fire" 265 cubic inch V8 in 1955.

Designated as *L98*, it replaced the *L83* "Cross-Fire Injection" engine that had been in the 1982 and 1984 cars—there were *no* 1983 Corvettes sold to the public because Chevrolet decided that

Lauren's high-tech for the mid-eighties and rather cool looking *L98* engine on display in May 2006

xiii

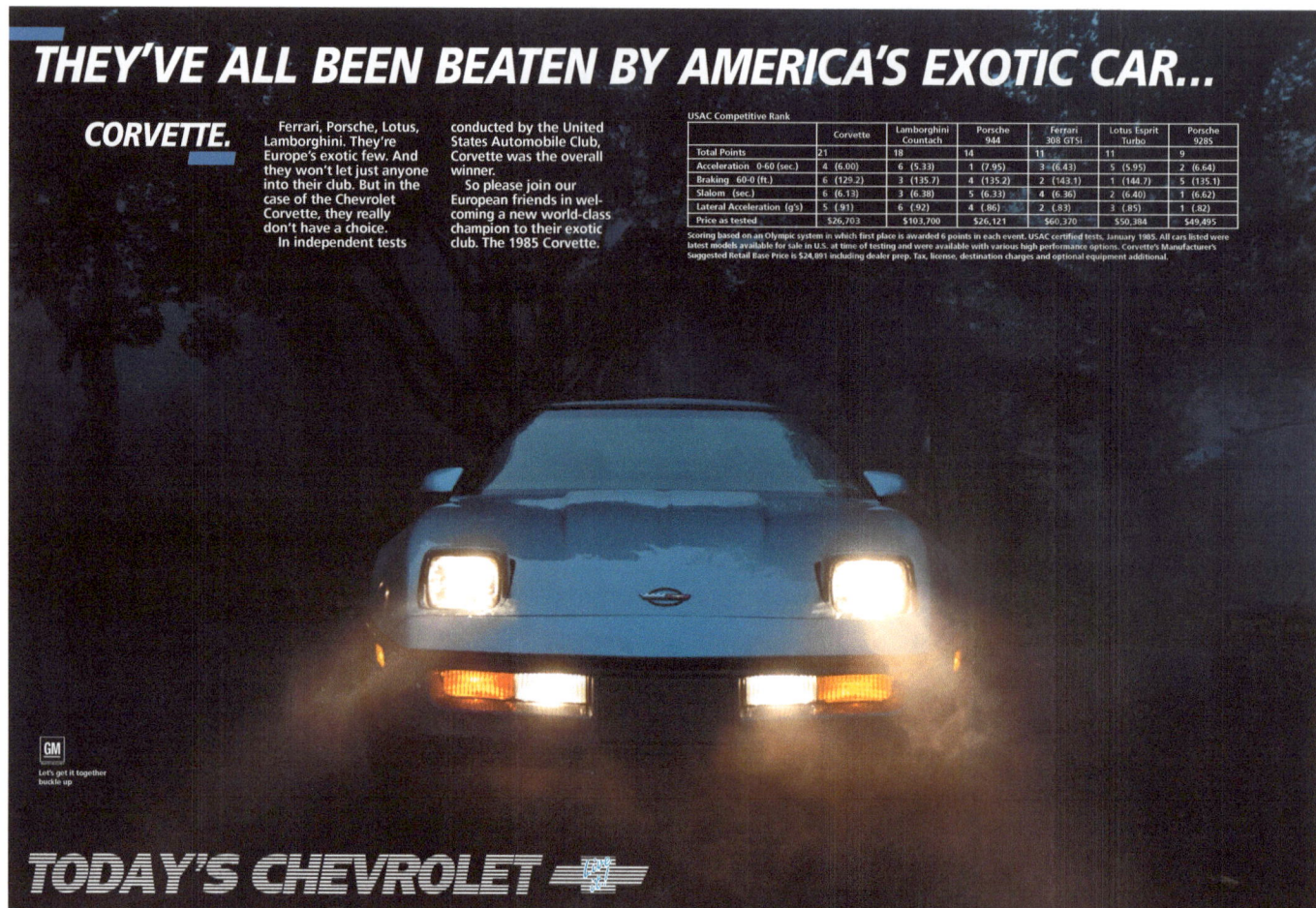

Replica advertisement to address one of my obsessions—I spent *way* too much time creating this over several years

the new-generation cars were not ready. This new "Tuned Port Injection" motor bumped net horsepower from 205 bhp to 230 bhp; younger readers will have to believe me that this was a pretty big deal in the more than a little horsepower-starved mid-1980s. The upgraded engine also managed to improve fuel economy to 16 city/22 highway by the standards of the day.

The improved engine certainly made the 1985 model significantly faster than the 1984 version in almost every way. Corvette engineers of the day proudly sported golf shirts that stated that "Life Begins At 150" (and there are still matching posters available) and a 1985 Corvette could just barely hit 150 mph if given enough time and a *lot* of distance. At the same time, the 0-60 mph time dropped about a second from around 6.6 seconds for the 1984 to around 5.6 seconds for the 1985—still reasonably spritely even today (though today's cars accelerate with far less drama). 1985 models also received many other refinements as Chevrolet's engineers reacted to some fairly aggressive feedback from the press and the public regarding the shortcomings of the all-new 1984s in real-world use. These changes made a difference: a review in the June 1984 issue of *Car and Driver* was sub-titled "Improving the vintage with careful aging."

1985 Corvette Equipment and Costs

By the standards of most cars in 1985—even compared to many high-end sports cars of that age—*Lauren* came *quite* well equipped. Every C4 Corvette came with air conditioning, power windows, power steering, power disc brakes, and a tilt and telescoping steering wheel. There was also a standard trip computer that's useful and still reasonably impressive even now, though it has some interesting memory limitations we didn't find out about until we were well into our trip.

The optional leather seats ($400) that *Lauren*'s first owner ordered were *all* leather (rare nowadays in anything but the highest end cars) and quite comfortable (though only the driver got even the option of six-way power seats and that went for an additional $215).

Gotta hook them while they're young—
a young man enjoying himself during a small show
at the Saratoga Auto Museum in June 2006

Lauren's car audio was a top of the line for 1985 Delco-GM/Bose music system option: an AM/FM stereo cassette player with four speakers carefully

matched to the particular layout of the Corvette's interior. This setup yielded marvelous and *very* expensive ($895!) sound for the mid-Eighties and is still reasonably serviceable now, at least when it is working correctly (and *Lauren*'s does after more than a little massaging).

In many areas, Chevrolet spared little expense with the early C4s. Here are three quick examples:

1) the aluminum alloy forged front control arms are gorgeous pieces of industrial art and never seem to fail (they're now quite popular in heavily customized hot rods)
2) the excellent brake calipers were outsourced to South Africa's Girlock instead of going the much more organizationally easy route and getting calipers from somewhere inside General Motors
3) there are an extravagant three separate switches for opening the glass rear hatch (Chevrolet saved a dollar or two on later C4s by removing the switch on the passenger door)

None of this impressive equipment and capability came at all cheap. Despite being Chevrolets and thus theoretically part of the Detroit manufacturer's traditional "low-priced three," Corvettes have *never* been inexpensive cars. They debuted at $3,744.55 in 1953—a lofty and aspirational price when every other Chevrolet model's base price was between $1,524 (about 41% of the Corvette) and $2,273 (61%). This sticker meant that the very first Corvettes cost as much as or more than some Austin-Healeys, Cadillacs, Lincolns, Packards, and Porsches of the day. Eighties Corvettes were even pricier in constant dollars—*Lauren*'s base price with destination charge was $24,878 (approximately $58,800 in 2018 dollars).

After adding the aforementioned Z_{51} performance handling package, Delco-GM/Bose music system, leather seats, and six-way power driver's seat, along with power door locks ($170), a transparent targa roof panel ($595), performance axle ratio (a bargain at $22 but required because the Z_{51} had been ordered), cruise control ($185), and rear window and side mirror defoggers ($160), *Lauren* stickered for a decidedly non-trivial $27,990. This price is about $66,200 in today's funds and not at all far from what a decently equipped 2019 Corvette Stingray coupe with the Z_{51} performance package costs more than thirty years later—with precisely twice the horsepower.

Lauren was born on November 16, 1984, in Bowling Green, Kentucky, which has been the only Corvette assembly plant location since the end of the 1981 model year. A relatively early 1985 model year

Far too many reflections, but still a much-beloved photo: *Lauren* outside a local diner at 7:24 AM on her "arrival anniversary" celebration in March 2010

Corvette, she was shipped to Fred Bauer Chevrolet in the St. Johns neighborhood of Portland, Oregon. Fred Bauer was a well-known dealership for over 30 years, but all of its structures are long gone—it is now the location of an active food share, a large self-storage facility, and an abandoned garage. Over the next 19 years, *Lauren* would have three owners, all of them in Oregon, and she would travel 46,500 miles—a little under 2,500 miles a year.

Perhaps the Real Reason We Took This Trip

In early 2013 *Lauren* challenged me (I don't remember precisely how) as only a car that is not needed for any practical, useful, and rational purpose can, causing me to write this … screed on a couple of Corvette-centric Internet forums in May 2013. I quote it in its painful and unmodified entirety:

It's Not the Same as It Was in 2004 …

… I took the 1985 out for some miles today, and I noticed some things.

It's a more tenuous feeling taking her out than it was in 2004. Of course, that was 33,000 miles ago, but the car seems more … fragile. I'm mindful of all that sweat equity (mine and many others) in it and the knowledge that it is now so … old. Less and less early C4s on the road for any reason and she'll be thirty (!) years old in November 2014.

The car judges well and drives acceptably but the problems remain present and they are a litany: the "dumb as a bag of rocks" computer, the creaks and rattles in the interior, the passenger side power window near death, the console light that keeps slowly melting the console plastic, the seats and steering wheel not far from a recovery, the repaint that is who knows how many thousands of miles out, the characteristic droops on both front and rear bumpers that will need to be fixed with the repaint. They're known problems, and they can get fixed: but some of them (seats, repaint, bumpers) will require cubic dollars.

When I drive, the car feels small. All those larger and heavier vehicles around me seem to rarely look—and I have no airbags, no ABS, no traction control. Driving in heavy traffic (and there's so much of it around Philadelphia) accentuates the feeling of fragility. I look past those lovely thin A-pillars—the

ones that Dave Hill compared the C5's to and found the C5 wanting—and I know that the C5's are thicker and uglier because you can statically mount the car upside down on them. Those same lovely traits are repeated throughout the 1985: survival in an accident will come mostly by avoiding it in the first place.

So, the overall driving experience has changed a little for the worse, though the car is in much better shape than it was when it first came off that truck. Is this a new phase or the beginning of the end?

Just some thoughts.

Responses to this particular post on the various forums were, predictably, all over the place. Some of the many replies (stunningly) weren't that positive or reinforcing. My wife's reaction was both fantastic and wonderfully characteristic: "Do you still love that car?", Ivelis said. "Yes," I responded, more quickly than I thought I would. "We should take it on a long trip," she said, yet again knowing me better than I know myself.

I'll acknowledge right now that *Lauren* is not nearly as comfortable a long distance driver as our other Corvettes, so I figured my lovely wife would eventually come to her senses. However, I then caught the road tripping bug once again. Traveling the Lincoln Highway, which turned one hundred years old in 2013 (see what I'm doing with the book title?), seemed like a good change of pace from Route 66 (which we've traveled twice). When I brought up the Lincoln Highway as an idea, Ivelis readily and enthusiastically agreed (did I tell you that she is amazing?) and we were on.

Some Non-Trivial Vehicle Preparation

Preparing *Lauren* for a cross-country trip involved what I think of as "hardening" her for the longest journey she had driven, at least during the ten years we have owned her (the most extended trip we had previously taken was 2,723 miles in July 2008). After consulting with a few of the C4 experts we are privileged to know, I got to work. I removed the carefully prepared show battery (yes, crazy car people have such things) and a brand new Sears DieHard Gold—one of the best currently available batteries that is the correct size for a 1985 Corvette—replaced it. A modern and high-tech cotton air filter replaced the stock, judgeable, and downright primitive paper version. The aging Goodyear show tires were swapped out for modern, aggressive, and sticky BF Goodrich rubber sourced from our always helpful friends at TireRack.

At the same time, I checked the original and small "Space Saver" spare tire and made sure it was fully inflated. It would likely not get us far if we had a flat, but it and its carrier serve as part of the rear crumple zone in case of a collision.

We also did some far more significant maintenance than just the battery, air filter, and tires. A good friend of mine with a lot of C4 experience (thanks so very much for everything, John Porter!) and I spent several hours carefully cleaning the stylish but finicky engine throttle body intake, perhaps for the first time it had *ever* been cleaned.

I had *Lauren*'s air conditioning checked out since we expected to face at least some significant heat on our trip, but it tested out as fully functional. We also had the inside of the passenger door wholly rebuilt to better than new. Finally, some tiny holes in the rear exhaust pipes were identified and patched.

For Christmas 2013, my sister Helen, her husband Michael, and their wonderfully car-crazy (and I have the photos to prove it close at hand) little boy Julian gave us some C4-specific add-on cup holders—*Lauren*'s stock cup holders are nothing short of pathetic (like almost all sports car cup holders). At least we would have somewhere to put our coffee …

To get just a bit more comfort, I purchased (please don't laugh too much—I was willing to try absolutely *anything* short of actually switching vehicles) quite thick and utterly non-stock floor mats, hoping to attenuate at least a few of the 1985 Corvette's notorious vibrations.

In what may be an apparent preparation to some readers, Ivelis and I carefully tested which different pieces of our luggage would fit in the rear compartment along with all the other equipment we were carrying. Finally, we had *Lauren* professionally detailed both inside and out. The two of us figured she might as well look as good as possible for at least the beginning of our long distance jaunt.

There Must Be Appropriate Music

Music of all kinds has always been *vital* to us—it is a significant part of the story of how Ivelis and I first met and then fell in love. In part because of this, we took an approximately one-hundred-mile test run in our newly "hardened" *Lauren*, driving up to **Young Ones Records** in Kutztown, Pennsylvania to secure some 1985-appropriate cassette tapes to play on the Delco-GM/Bose music system.

We met with success, securing more than enough tapes to fill the eight slots in *Lauren*'s center console. The availability of thirty-year-old and correctly functioning used cassette tapes for purchase in mid-2014 seems to me to be a definite indication that the oft-discussed "long tail" of at least some of our commerce in the United States is remarkably long.

Planning for the Trip Itself

As I prepared for our journey, I quickly detected one critical difference between our Route 66 trips and this Lincoln Highway trip. There is nothing like the vast amount of written and online support that exists for the Mother Road (one could almost call it the "Route 66-industrial complex"). Even though the Lincoln Highway has recently celebrated its centennial, there are approximately three times the guides and references for Route 66 as there are for the Lincoln Highway. I sensed some real constraints in our available resources for this particular trip.

Ivelis is an excellent sport on these extended road trips of ours, but she does have a few requirements that she has adopted over our decades of taking long trips together. In general, she is willing to wake up and be on the road quite early in the day. However, she unquestionably wants more often than not to arrive at wherever we are staying for the night by 5:00 PM.

Since the Lincoln Highway is often less on the "beaten track" than the interstates and since we had just about *no idea* how far we would be able to travel each day, I prepared an extensive multi-page list of cities and towns where we could stop. This list included relevant motels, restaurants, gas stations, and other points of interest. I tried to have the possible stops no more than a half an hour separated. Where things got far more spread out as the route

Best laid plans: our theoretical Lincoln Highway route

moved to the mid-west and west, I explicitly noted how far apart those towns and cities were.

A couple of weeks before we were due to leave, Ivelis mentioned that it would probably be a good idea to add the many Chevrolet dealers located along the Lincoln Highway route to the list I was building. I didn't need any convincing, so I added those locations to the pages that I had already created. I ended up finding 51 dealers either on or very close to our intended route, the first being Chevrolet of Jersey City in (natch!) Jersey City, New Jersey and the last being Fairfield Chevrolet Subaru in Fairfield, California.

Our Specific Lincoln Highway Route

The Lincoln Highway's actual route from New York City to San Francisco changed notably over the few decades that the highway was a "going concern." Thus, folks who wish to follow a correct route have some legitimate options. A few of these can modify the journey significantly.

Ivelis and I decided fairly early in our rather extensive planning for this particular trip that we would default to the newest version of the route. This route is what the Lincoln Highway Association refers to in its very detailed maps and excellent documentation on the Internet as "third generation re-alignments (until 1928)." Our thoughts when making this decision were three (in no particular order):

a) the average road on the third generation re-alignment would (hopefully) be at least somewhat more open, current, and comfortable than the various older alignments—though we didn't know whether this was generally true (and the folks we asked had no definitive answer)
b) the third generation route is at least a little shorter (by about 250 miles), and we unquestionably had time constraints, mostly because both of us were working full-time when we took this trip
c) only the third generation route passes anywhere near the famous and historic Bonneville Salt Flats in Utah, which has been on our automobile related "bucket list" for many years

Significant Concerns Remain

In spite of the many preparations I have described, both Ivelis and I were quite aware that there were many unknowns on this trip, including whether we would even complete it successfully. This situation was something that had not been true of our two previous "Big Trips" back and forth across the United States. The possibility of a catastrophic failure of some essential system in this particular Corvette was part of an honest and realistic assessment of our plans. A few of our friends heightened this awareness: they were quite enthused by our trip—until they figured out that we were driving it on our own.

We started our journey with only one known problem (though I assumed that there were likely many issues that I didn't know about). While doing a last thorough check on the Sunday of the weekend before we were starting our trip, I discovered that the long problematic cigarette lighter (there were absolutely no pretensions of calling it "accessory power" in 1985) had failed yet again.

After some pained consideration, I decided not to rip apart most of *Lauren*'s almost entirely plastic dash (the majority of which is notably brittle after nearly thirty years) with only one week to go (and very likely break some other things deep inside the car). Ivelis and I agreed that we could "rough it" through each day with no onboard power charging for our assortment of Apple-branded electronics, which included a MacBook Pro Retina 13-inch, an iPad mini, and two iPhones.

Staging to Manhattan
Bryn Mawr, Pennsylvania to New York City, New York

Saturday, May 17, 2014, came quickly. In the mid-morning the two of us carefully loaded *Lauren*'s surprisingly spacious (almost 18 cubic feet) rear storage compartment completely full under the luggage shade that is nicer and far more integrated than what you get with even the newest Corvettes—don't get Ivelis or me started about that! We packed every available nook and cranny in the back of the car with luggage, tools, and supplies as I tried to account for at least the most probable eventualities on this riskiest of our many "Big Trips."

Starting mileage—71,146 and change

Heading for the Eastern Terminus
After a final check or two, we departed from our home in Bryn Mawr, Pennsylvania. Once we had traversed a few local roads, we drove up to New York City via first the Pennsylvania Turnpike and then the New Jersey Turnpike on what turned out to be a lovely spring afternoon—definitely a good sign at the start of this long and potentially fraught trip. As I had hoped, it was generally "smooth sailing" on this particular Saturday as we drove slightly over 100 miles. Ivelis and I encountered our only significant traffic issues during the day as we traversed the many merges (including **The Helix**—yes, a merge with an actual name) into the **Lincoln Tunnel** before it deposited us right into the center of Manhattan on West 38th Street.

Relatively quick "staging" from Bryn Mawr, Pennsylvania to New York City, New York

Immensely motivating banner for the new Corvette Stingray as we near Times Square

From there, we drove along 42nd Street through **Times Square** itself toward our hotel. On our way through "The Crossroads of the World," we passed a giant billboard advertising the (at that point) almost brand new 2014 Corvette Stingray—very cool and definitely another good omen. I would eagerly search for any positive indicator I could find throughout this trip.

One of the Greatest Hotels in the World
That night in New York, we stayed (on a few years worth of Hilton points—please don't be that impressed) at the always-wonderful **Waldorf Astoria** hotel. Opened in 1931, the Waldorf Astoria is a large, ornate, and thoroughly stunning complex that occupies an entire city block enclosed by Park Avenue, Lexington Avenue, 49th Street, and 50th Street. Our biggest issue during our entire stay turned out to be that

Snazzy motor lobby that it took us a little while to find

we couldn't immediately find the motor lobby—we realized after finally getting to it that we had never previously driven to the hotel (our earlier visits had been via foot, taxi, or car service).

Happily, once we actually managed to arrive, the two of us were quickly and courteously valeted and checked in to this magnificent hotel. Ivelis and I then headed upstairs and got settled in our notably large for New York City "superior" room—I have always believed that space is the ultimate luxury in "the city that never sleeps." Afterward, the two of us headed back down on one of the Waldorf Astoria's many swift elevators. Ivelis and I each had an excellent celebratory kick-off Manhattan (of course!) at the **Peacock Alley Bar & Lounge** in the lovely Art Deco grand lobby.

Excellent Manhattan at the Peacock Alley Bar

Checking off a Longtime Dining Goal

For dinner, we walked just a few blocks east and south over to the original (and rather small) **Palm** restaurant, which opened in 1926 at 837 Second Avenue and has been there ever since. Every Palm we have been to has caricatures on their walls, but this restaurant is where that idea got started—many of the drawings are by famous cartoonists who worked at the nearby King Features Syndicate on 235 East 45th Street.

I have been trying to go to dinner at that particular location for years but have never made reservations far enough ahead of time to actually get in. Our dinner was quite good, though in the end not notably different from the 25 or so other Palms that are now scattered across America.

After our dinner at the Palm, Ivelis and I strolled, hand in hand, and very happily around the Turtle Bay area of Manhattan. During our late spring saunter, we stopped to view the iconic **United Nations** complex. Alfred Hitchcock's excellent, surprisingly funny, and remarkably influential—just look at any early James Bond movie—film *North by Northwest* came immediately to mind as we walked by. Next on our route came the magnificent Art Deco **Chrysler Building** (even today still the tallest brick building in the world). The two of us stopped for just one more cocktail at **The Capital Grille** in the Chrysler Center complex on 42nd Street before returning to the hotel in the late evening for a good night's sleep—the walls are nice and thick in the luxurious Waldorf Astoria.

Looking way up at the handsome Chrysler Building

The Way Out, Part I
New York City, New York to Warsaw, Indiana

The morning drive from New York City to Coatesville, Pennsylvania

On Sunday morning, May 18th, the alarms on both of our smartphones went off quite early for most Mulhern weekends: 6:00 AM. There was a good reason for this quick start—my best estimate was that we would need to drive about 390 miles on this day in what I knew would be unpredictable and likely somewhat congested (even on a Sunday) east coast traffic. A bit tense and quite excited, we showered, dressed, and checked out reasonably quickly but somewhat reluctantly from the marvelous and unique Waldorf Astoria.

Two of the very proficient and quite personable parking valets in the hotel's stylish motor court clucked over both of us and also (somewhat surprisingly to us) over *Lauren* as we re-packed the car, got ourselves situated, and prepared to leave. Ivelis and I certainly got the sense that a valeted 1985 Corvette was very much not a typical vehicle at the Waldorf Astoria in 2014.

And Here We Go!

At about 7:00 AM, we departed the Waldorf Astoria and drove to Times Square, which is the official eastern terminus of the Lincoln Highway. We experienced the expected light weekend traffic but also noticed (perhaps because we were really keyed-up) what seemed to be fairly awful even for New York City streets—*Lauren*'s aging (old) and aged (many miles) chassis creaked and groaned even more than it usually does.

When we arrived at Times Square itself (our precise starting point was 47th and Broadway), I slammed *Lauren*'s long-suffering *THM 700-R4* (the THM stands for Turbo Hydra-Matic—a General Motors trademark dating all the way back to 1964) automatic transmission into park. Next, I wrenched the long and substantial driver's side door open and dashed across 47th Street to take a few of the all-important "beginning of the trip" pictures. If you look extremely carefully at the photograph on the following page, you might be able to sense Ivelis waiting just a little impatiently in the passenger's seat as *Lauren*'s "Tuned Port Injection" engine rumbled as it idled—making the entire car twitch.

After leaving Times Square, it was off toward the west side of Manhattan. Early Lincoln Highway

Where it begins: early Sunday morning, Times Square, New York City

motorists took the New York Central's steam ferry across the Hudson River from 42nd Street to Weehawken, New Jersey—the NY Waterway company runs a similar route today, but its modern boats do not carry any vehicle larger than a bicycle. Instead of traveling across the surface of the river, we took an almost empty one and a half miles in the Lincoln Tunnel about 100 feet underneath the Hudson to Union City. It seemed that our plan of leaving Manhattan quite early on a Sunday morning was working out!

Once in New Jersey, we did have just a little bit of trouble picking up the correct route in Jersey City—there were many turns to navigate after exiting the tunnel. After a little uncertainty, we began to head southwest along first the JFK Boulevard in Newark and then joined New Jersey State Route 27 in Elizabeth. Almost as soon as Ivelis and I became confident that  we had regained our bearings, both of us simultaneously noticed that it was turning out to be a rather lovely morning.

As we drove along the highway, the two of us were also beginning to adjust once again to long distance travel in the relatively tight interior of our 1985 coupe compared to our other Corvettes. Ivelis and I were also slowly figuring out where to best stow our various electronics and analog references, as storage is very sparse in the passenger compartment of an early C4. There is no traditional glove box on the passenger side (a "bread box" padded passive restraint system occupies that area)—only a medium-sized center console originally designed to hold eight cassette tapes, the owner's manual, and a few odd and ends.

Remaining on Route 27, we stopped for two quick coffees at a fast food restaurant in the city of Rahway (childhood home of Nobel Prize-winning economist Milton Friedman). Afterward, we proceeded on through the unincorporated community of Iselin—known to many (including a very young John) as Metropark, after the train station built in 1971 to serve the then new *Metroliner* trains. Next came the borough of Metuchen (birthplace of illusionist David Copperfield), the township of Edison, the city of New Brunswick, and the borough of Princeton. In Princeton, Route 27 ends. We drove along US Route 206 for a few miles before joining a portion of the almost 2,400-mile-long US Route 1 just before stopping in the village of Lawrenceville for breakfast.

View straight up through the tinted targa top on a beautiful May day

Our First Diner of the Trip

We ate a tasty and filling meal at **Michael's Family Restaurant & Diner** in Lawrenceville, the first of several great diners the two of us sampled (perhaps more than a little *too* enthusiastically!) as we traveled along the Lincoln Highway. After we had

The Way Out, Part I

finished eating, we got back in *Lauren* and drove along US Route 1 through the downtown of the city of Trenton.

We took the **Trenton-Morrisville Toll Bridge** across the Delaware River into Pennsylvania. Only a few hundred feet to our right as we crossed over the river was the **Lower Trenton Bridge,** with the famous "Trenton Makes, the World Takes" lettering first installed in 1935 (the signage is much clearer in the evening).

"Trenton Makes, the World Takes"

After crossing the river into Pennsylvania, the first place we entered was the borough of Morrisville. Only five miles to the south at this point on our route was the borough of Bristol, home of Contemporary Corvette, a Corvette-specific junkyard that has often been very helpful to us as we restored *Lauren*. We proceeded along US Route 1 through large portions of northeast and north Philadelphia. Instead of taking Broad Street south and following the original route, we stayed on Route 1 and crossed the Schuylkill River on the Twin Bridges. Shortly thereafter, we took a right at the intersection of Route 1 and US Route 30 in the unincorporated community of Wynnewood (birthplace of Eighties rock singer Joan Jett) and left the Philadelphia city line. For the first time in our trip (but certainly not the last) we began driving almost due west. First, we drove through the unincorporated community of Ardmore—until the 1950s home of the Autocar truck company, an early corporate supporter of the Lincoln Highway (they donated two trucks to install those distinctive road markers). Also for the first time on our trip, we began to closely parallel railroad tracks—in this case, the Pennsylvania Railroad's famous "Main Line" from Philadelphia to Pittsburgh.

A Quick Stop Back Home

This jaunt was the first of the *many* long road trips that we have taken where the two of us passed by our house somewhere in the middle of the journey, and that certainly felt a little strange. After driving through Haverford, we made a planned stop at our home in Bryn Mawr for a quick bathroom break and to secure a few supplies that we had somehow neglected to pack just one day before.

After about 20 minutes, we once again left our house in Bryn Mawr. We enjoyed a smooth ride along US Route 30 through the unincorporated

The mid-day drive from Coatesville, Pennsylvania to Fort Louden, Pennsylvania

New York City, New York to Warsaw, Indiana

communities of Villanova, Wayne (named after United States Army General "Mad" Anthony Wayne from the American Revolutionary War), and Devon (home of the Devon Horse Show since 1896, the oldest outdoor multi-breed horse competition in the United States).

Gorgeous late 1960s Chevrolet pickup truck waiting in busy traffic in Villanova, Pennsylvania

Next came the boroughs of Malvern and Downingtown, Thorndale, and the city of Coatesville. We then drove through the unincorporated community of Sadsburyville, the town of Gap (the intersection of many old local highways), and the town of Kinzers. After that came Paradise—described many years ago by *Ward's Quarterly* as a "delightfully named town." We passed through the unincorporated community of Soudersburg and the small town of Ronks as we headed into the charming center of

Shoo-fly pies and "Amish Stuff" call to us (but we resist somehow) at the circa 1946 Dutch Haven store in Ronks, Pennsylvania

Appropriately named Route 30 Diner— a 1959 Silk City just east of Lancaster, Pennsylvania

the city of Lancaster. Lancaster also includes the world's oldest Goodyear dealer—a suitable place for *Lauren* to visit back when you could still buy the original stock "Gatorback" tires (don't get me started on finding tires for an early C4).

NOT GOING EXACTLY ACCORDING TO PLAN

As we exited Lancaster and began heading west toward the city of York, we encountered our first of the several times along this trip when we were forced to leave our chosen Lincoln Highway route for a notable amount of time and distance. In this case, it was because of some fairly substantial road construction that I must admit was reasonably best scheduled for the weekend. Making the first of many snap decisions on this trip, we turned northwest in the borough of Columbia (home of the National Watch and Clock Museum) and followed State Route 441 for about 45 minutes.

Because of this unexpected change in our route, we missed a few interesting Lincoln Highway stops we had been hoping to see in central Pennsylvania, including the aforementioned York, the town of Thomasville, and the boroughs of Abbottstown (with its circa 1953 **Lincoln Speedway** ⅜-mile banked clay race track) and New Oxford. We ended up driving almost all of the way northwest to the Pennsylvania state capital of Harrisburg before we were finally able to turn back southwest along US Route 15. We rejoined the Lincoln Highway at a point only a few miles east of the borough of Gettysburg.

On our first day on the Lincoln Highway, we were already on track to travel much more miles than I initially expected, so things clearly weren't

That dreaded fuel reserve warning

going exactly to plan—something I had anticipated but was hoping wouldn't happen on this particular (already long) day. After rejoining our planned route, we stopped at a Sheetz gas station just outside of Gettysburg to fill an almost completely empty fuel tank. *Lauren*'s digital instrument cluster was showing the dreaded C4 fuel reserve warning, which experience (and many warnings from others with similar Corvettes) tells us means to get more gasoline *right now*. By the way, there really is a Sheetz family—though the name sounds like the work of some hard-working marketing team, it is not an invented one; Bob Sheetz started the company in 1952.

There's so much history in these Gettysburg fields

Lovely and Historic Gettysburg

After our fuel stop, we drove slowly through Lincoln Square right in the center of beautiful (and so historic) Gettysburg along US Route 30. The two of us have visited Gettysburg many times (and it isn't that far from where we live), so we didn't make a stop there on this particular trip. It is, however, impossible to view the often-lovely scenery in this part of Pennsylvania without some degree of enhanced awareness of the presence of history.

Ivelis and I exited the middle of Gettysburg and headed west-northwest toward Chambersburg. On our way out of town, we passed along the green farm fields where the Confederate Third Corps of General A.P. Hill attacked the three corps of General John F. Reynolds during the first of the three days of the Battle of Gettysburg, which was just over 150 years ago on July 1st, 1863. I join many others in believing that Gettysburg was almost certainly the most important and decisive battle in the American Civil War.

Lauren parked outside the 30 West Family Restaurant in Chambersburg, Pennsylvania

We drove on first through the tiny unincorporated community of McKnightstown (population 226) and then the borough of Chambersburg. With efficient service from a friendly and competent waitress, we ate a late lunch at the small and quiet **30 West Family Restaurant** located just west of Chambersburg.

One of many Lincoln Highway reassurance markers—this one is in Fort Loudon, Pennsylvania

New York City, New York to Warsaw, Indiana

Around this time of the day, we began to see many more Lincoln Highway reassurance markers than earlier—though we didn't need them, at least this early on our trip. "See," I said to Ivelis as *Lauren*'s engine rumbled happily along the lovely roads in the beautiful weather, "we're actually on the right route." She giggled.

After our meal, we entered a small part of the Appalachian Mountains, pressing on through the town of Breezewood and the borough of Everett (birthplace of author Dean Koontz). Next came the pretty and friendly little borough of Bedford—home to a circa 1933 Gulf station still owned by the family that first built it. Just to the south of Bedford is the large, lovely, and palatial Bedford Springs Resort, which dates from 1809 and completed a full restoration in 2007.

Two Points of Attraction in a Tiny Town

Next up on the Lincoln Highway was the little borough of Schellsburg (population 387). Schellsburg had two major points of interest for us—one very much still in existence and one that has been gone for over a decade. The point of interest still around is the cool Lincoln Highway mural painted on the side of one of the Bison Corral's barns.

Lincoln Highway mural on the side of a Bison Corral barn in Schellsburg, Pennsylvania

Dunkle's Gulf in Bedford, Pennsylvania

The place to visit that is no more was the **Grand View Hotel** (also known as the Ship Hotel), which was built in 1927 and heavily modified to look considerably more ship-like in 1932. It spent many decades as a going concern before it burned down completely in 2001 after (ugh) an extended period

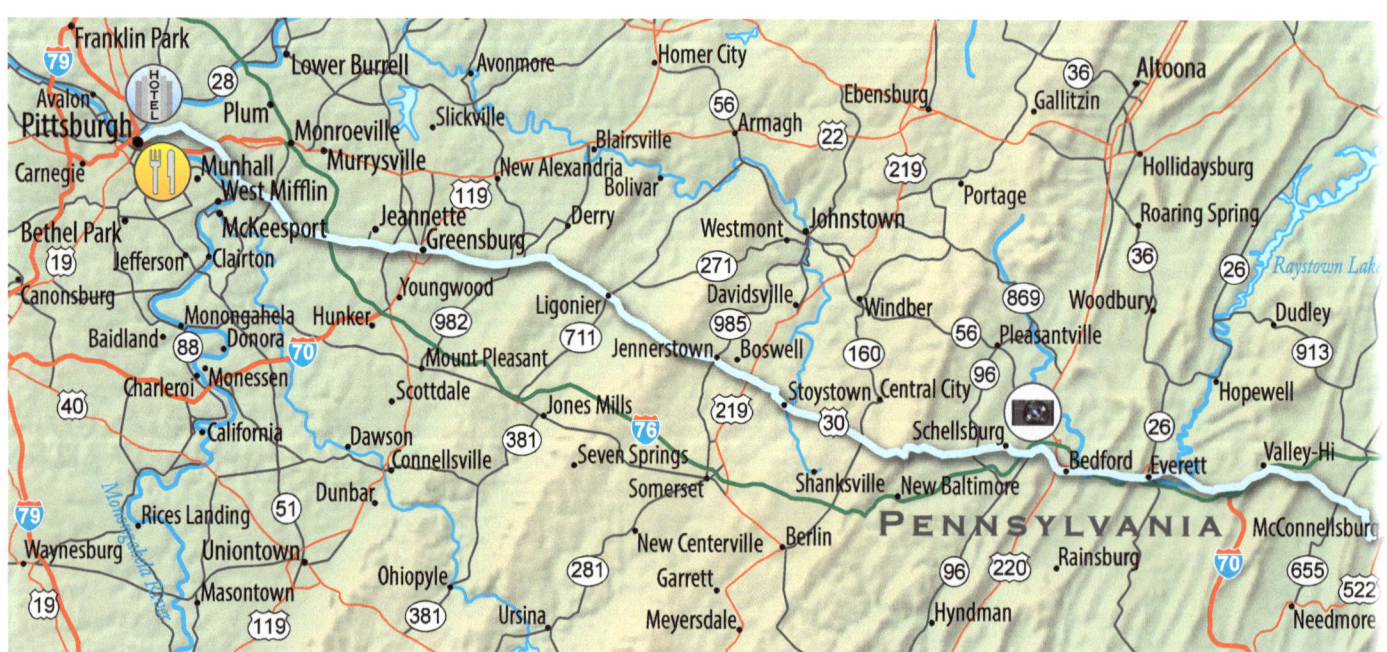

The afternoon drive from Fort Louden, Pennsylvania to Pittsburgh, Pennsylvania

of neglect. For all those years, many claimed that the hotel's view from Mount Ararat (2,656 feet at its peak) let lucky guests see three states and seven counties.

Some things aren't around to visit any more —the Grand View Hotel burned down in 2001

Missing a chance to at least see this landmark by "only" thirteen years (the two of us didn't know enough to stop back then when we were relatively close) was a sharp reminder to both of us that our particular Lincoln Highway experience was merely a set of data points at a given time. What exists on this and, indeed, all historic routes is and will be ever-changing.

After our somewhat chastening pause in Schellsburg, we drove on through the boroughs of Jennerstown, Ligonier (named after French-born British Field Marshal John Ligonier—somebody with an exceptionally non-standard career path), and Youngstown, and the city of Greensburg as we headed northwest. We drove through the suburban borough of Wilkinsburg and headed toward downtown Pittsburgh. *Lauren* was running well even in the hilly Pennsylvania terrain (and getting surprisingly good gas mileage—about two miles per gallon over what I had expected), and our spirits were high as we neared the end of our first day on the Lincoln Highway.

Our Second Stay in Pittsburgh

After a few challenging turns (and one scary one—suffering from a loss of situational awareness due to some fatigue, I didn't see a mid-size crossover that I should have) in Pittsburgh's city center, we arrived spent but happy at our hotel at about 6:30 PM. We had traveled approximately 415 miles on our first full day—about 25 miles and perhaps half an hour longer than expected because of our radical detour around the construction near York.

Pittsburgh was our planned destination for our first night on the Lincoln Highway. It was the only stopping place we had scheduled and reserved until our expected arrival in San Francisco—more than 2,600 miles away from Pittsburgh by the most direct route (which we were absolutely not traveling). At this point in our travels, we didn't even know what day the two of us would arrive on the left coast, primarily because we had little idea of how many miles we would be able to cover each day. We did hope to do better than the circa 1924 *A Complete Official Road Guide to the Lincoln Highway* indicates, which is that about 100 miles are "a moderate day's drive."

In Pittsburgh, we stayed in a ridiculously large "Signature" room on the twelfth floor of the marvelous circa 1916 **Omni William Penn**, which is on the National Register of Historic Places (I'll state right up front that we stopped at a lot of locations on the National Register during this trip). By 1929, this stately and gorgeous hotel was one of the largest in the world, with 1,600 rooms. Just one year later a gala held at the hotel for the governors of Ohio, Pennsylvania, and West Virginia celebrated the opening of the Lincoln Highway in their respective states—so this was certainly an appropriate place to stay. Omni's current configuration (they've owned the hotel since 2001) has a "mere" 567 rooms.

Omni William Penn hotel in Pittsburgh, Pennsylvania

We had stayed at the William Penn once before in April 2003 as we brought our Corvette convertible home from the Bowling Green Assembly Plant and the National Corvette Museum in Bowling

Green, Kentucky. I did warn Ivelis before we left on this particular trip that the William Penn was quite likely to be the *last* nice hotel we would be staying in until we made it all the way across the United States to San Francisco.

Looking toward "The Taking of Fort Pitt" mural in The Terrace Room at the Omni William Penn

We got comfortably settled in our huge room, and I sent a quick and generally positive update to the online forums that were following us on our trip along the Highway. After Ivelis had taken a quick snapshot of our hotel room number—a smart idea on a long road trip when all those numbers can start to blend together—we took one of their Otis elevators back downstairs. The two of us ate a diverting and enjoyable dinner in the lovely, ornate, and striking **The Terrace Room** restaurant (known as The Italian Terrace when the hotel first opened), which is located right off the impressive main lobby of the hotel.

After dinner, we repaired to **The Tap Room** (one of the quite large William Penn's three bars), where we had some excellent mixed drinks (a Champagne Cobbler, a Blackberry Sour, and a Royal Manhattan, if you must know—along with two large bottles of sparkling water). We also had an enjoyable, interesting, and relaxed (though he was working hard) conversation with Bob Harah, one of the bartenders working there on that particular evening.

Day Two on the Lincoln Highway

After a good night's rest in that enormous and comfortable hotel room that I have previously mentioned, we woke up, showered, dressed, and prepared to depart the hospitable William Penn. After packing and checking out, Ivelis and I waited patiently for the hotel's valets to bring us our car. They mistakenly brought us a late model Infiniti sedan first (!), so I'm willing to bet that the two of us didn't quite fit the profile of folks driving a 29-year-old Corvette. While we waited just a little while longer for *Lauren* to arrive, I used the extra time to take a few pictures of what was once was the Alcoa building (completed in 1953 and still sporting its striking original all-aluminum façade) and has been repurposed as the Regional Enterprise Tower.

Soon, Ivelis and I pulled away from the hotel, heading along Cherry Way and Grant Street. It just happened that we left Pittsburgh during the morning rush hour—traffic was quite heavy (it was a Monday), but not terrible. We crossed the Monongahela River

The morning drive from Pittsburgh, Pennsylvania to Wooster, Ohio

The Way Out, Part I

Quick photo of the amazing (formerly) Alcoa building as we prepare to leave Pittsburgh

on the double decker **Fort Pitt Bridge**, which more than a few commentators note for its many and challenging lane changes. We certainly experienced this particular traffic issue— *Lauren*'s aging powertrain responded unhappily to the continuous fits and starts of traffic as I worked rather hard to position her in the appropriate lanes.

Exiting the Pittsburgh metropolitan area was one of the first times that our "modern" 1928 route varied substantially from the original 1914 route, in this case for about forty miles. Instead of heading northwest along the Ohio River, we headed out in a more westerly direction along or quite near to US Route 30 through the borough of Crafton (birthplace of former Pittsburgh Steelers head coach Bill Cowher) and the unincorporated community of Imperial. In Imperial, we stopped for a quiet and filling breakfast at one of the many Pittsburgh-area **Kings Family Restaurants** (around since 1967 and named after a real person named King). A little further along the highway in the unincorporated community of Clinton, I managed to take a few wrong turns before the two of us successfully got back on course.

We then passed through a very short (three-mile) portion of West Virginia at the most northern tip of that state. This brief stretch includes the small city of Chester (named after J. Chester McDonald, one of the city's original planners) and its famous 14-foot tall **World's Largest Teapot**, dating from 1938 and recently restored.

Crossing the Ohio River into East Liverpool, Ohio

Traffic began to open up and become at least somewhat easier to navigate. We traveled across the **Jennings Randolph Bridge** (at about *three times* the recommended 250-foot maximum length, the largest Platt truss bridge in all of America), crossing the Ohio River into Ohio into the city of East Liverpool, and rejoining the older Lincoln Highway alignments. We passed through East Liverpool (once known as the "Pottery

World's Largest Teapot in Chester, West Virginia

Passing by (but not actually stopping at) the Street Trolley Diner (a 1956 O'Mahony) in Lisbon, Ohio

New York City, New York to Warsaw, Indiana

The mid-day drive from Wooster, Ohio to just east of Lima, Ohio

Capital of the World") fairly quickly and proceeded steadily northwest on another pretty day (on these first few days we were having splendid luck with the weather), heading through the villages of Lisbon and Hanoverton.

The Old Route Makes Its Presence Felt

In Ohio, we had what I think of as one of our first truly defining Lincoln Highway experiences during the trip. We stopped mid-morning for a few at least somewhat stylish pictures (I realize after our trip that I parked *Lauren* in a strikingly sub-optimal location for a superior photo) at a tiny and lovely gas station in the center of the village of Minerva. Located at the intersection of the Lincoln Highway and Market Street, the station is quite old: built around 1910, it predates the Lincoln Highway itself by a few years (the first purpose-built gas station is only five years older).

Parked behind the antique gas pumps at a very old gas station in Minerva, Ohio

This gas station was also a Lincoln Highway "Control Point"—a place where early travelers could safely reset their often less than accurate trip odometers as they followed detailed directions that were often written by the tenths of a mile. In my copy of *A Complete Official Road Guide to the Lincoln Highway*, Minerva is listed as 85.8 miles from Pittsburgh and 16.2 miles from Canton, and I'm advised that I can expect the road to be the then still current macadam.

The "For Sale" sign posted at that old station gave both of us more than a little concern for its future—hopefully, someone will come along soon with another and perhaps more successful business plan to keep this classic gas station around for another hundred years.

After our short stop in Minerva, we continued driving west for several quite scenic hours on the well-maintained two-lane highway, passing through the city of Canton, the village of Dalton, and the cities of Wooster and Mansfield.

Mail Pouch Tobacco advertising painted on an old barn a few miles west of Minerva, Ohio

In the city of Bucyrus (which identifies itself as the "Bratwurst Capital of America" and hosts an annual three-day bratwurst festival every August), we paused for a few minutes to fuel *Lauren* with premium gasoline at a quietly welcoming Shell on Sandusky Avenue. The 1985 Corvette owner's manual explicitly states that she's *supposed* only to want plus (reasonable even for a sports car in the

The afternoon drive from Lima, Ohio to Warsaw, Indiana

mid-1980s), but we would learn later on this trip that she unquestionably prefers premium. After refueling, we moved on through the village of Nevada (named after the Sierra Nevada mountains) and the small city of Upper Sandusky. Somewhere along the way, we started following a striking red Series 3 Jaguar E-Type convertible—definitely automotive "eye candy" even if it was on a trailer.

Following an early 1970s Jaguar V12 E-Type (unfortunately on a trailer) a little east of Lima, Ohio

A Late but Really Great Lunch at Kewpee

It was getting well into mid-afternoon; we had yet to eat lunch, and I was getting famished; I have discovered over the last ten years of ownership that driving *Lauren* for long distances takes a lot of energy. Luckily, Ivelis was telling me with some enthusiasm that our next stop was going to be at a great classic burger place mentioned in one of our guides—and she turned out to be utterly correct.

Again, we headed slightly southwest from our relatively "modern" Lincoln Highway route for **Kewpee** on North Elizabeth Street in the downtown part of the city of Lima. The Kewpee chain dates from 1923—one of their many slogans is "Your Granpappy ate here." At its peak immediately before World War II there were approximately 400 locations in the United States; after an extended period of decline, there are now only five stores left, with three of them located in Lima (there's also one each in Lansing, Michigan and Racine, Wisconsin).

Classic and wonderful fast food burgers are still available inside this Kewpee in Lima, Ohio

Both of us loved Kewpee's service (courteous and supremely competent ladies of a certain age), their general straightforward and honest atmosphere inside that small but busy building, and (of course) their hamburgers. This was simple, almost

New York City, New York to Warsaw, Indiana

homemade American fast food, and delicious. I believe the two of us will be back someday, hopefully fairly soon—and a recent check with Ivelis tells me that she very definitely agrees.

After Ivelis and I had eaten our fill at Kewpee, we drove northwest through the village of Elida (birthplace of landscape artist Floyd Gahman) and rejoined our slightly more modern Lincoln Highway route near the small city of Delphos.

"Seedling Miles"

We proceeded through the city of Van Wert and the village of Convoy (named after a village in County Donegal, Ireland). A little bit west of Convoy, Ivelis and I drove over the location of one of the early Lincoln Highway demonstration "seedling miles" (also called the "Ideal Section"). In 1920, the first Lincoln Highway Association (LHA) decided to develop a section of road that would be adequate not only for the traffic of the day but also for highway transportation over the following two decades. The LHA assembled many of the country's leading roadway experts for lengthy meetings in December 1920 and February 1921 to decide on the design details of the Ideal Section. Some features agreed upon were:

1) A 100-foot right-of-way
2) A 40-foot wide concrete pavement 10 inches thick, making four 10-foot wide lanes
3) Curves with a minimum radius of 1,000 feet, with guardrails along all embankments
4) Banked curves designed for a speed of 35 miles per hour
5) A footpath for pedestrians
6) No grade crossings or advertising signs

Flat land as we enter Indiana

Shortly after passing the seedling mile location, we crossed over into Indiana, passing through the city of New Haven, and driving on through the rather familiar (to us) city of Fort Wayne.

After Fort Wayne, the slightly newer route separates yet again from the original route, once again closely paralleling the Pennsylvania Railroad's tracks. Instead of heading northwest towards South Bend, we drove west through Columbia City. We passed a 1995 Starlite diner (yes—they were still making them in 1995) a few miles further west along the highway. After that, we stopped for a quiet night at (I'll admit it) a national chain motel in the city of Warsaw (named after the capital of Poland), where authors Ambrose Bierce and Theodore Dreiser both went to high school. We had a relaxed but far more generic dinner than our lunch had been before turning in for the night. Our total mileage for the day had been about 350 miles, with only a couple of short detours.

Early that evening, our friend Jordan checked in via text from San Francisco. What follows is a relevant snippet of the conversation:

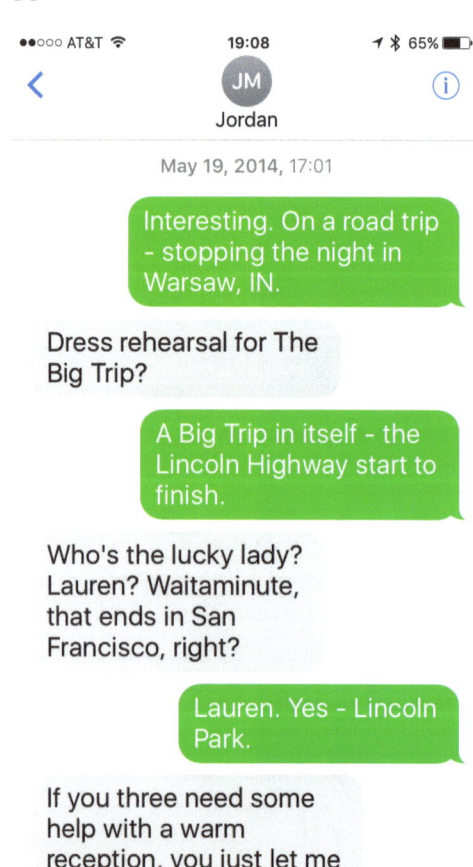

The Way Out, Part II
Warsaw, Indiana to North Platte, Nebraska

The early morning drive from Warsaw, Indiania to Matteson, Illinois

Early on a Tuesday morning in late May, Ivelis and I woke up, showered, dressed, did just a bit of re-packing, and departed from our reasonably comfortable motel in Warsaw, Indiana. After just a few turns, we rejoined US Route 30 and headed west-northwest through the unincorporated community of Atwood, the town of Etna Green (named after the township that it resides in), and the town of Bourbon. Bourbon is unquestionably an interesting, though not entirely uncommon name for a place to live—there are three communities and two counties so identified in the United States alone.

Unusual and distinctive name for a town

Country Driving in Northwestern Indiana

Next, the two of us proceeded through the cities of Plymouth—home of the annual Marshall County Blueberry Festival every September (I am a serious blueberry fan, so that sounds like a fun event). After that came the unincorporated community of Hanna and the town of Hamlet (named after the person who established the town and *not* a particular prince).

In the city of Valparaiso (named after the much larger Chilean port city of Valparaíso) we rejoined the oldest Lincoln Highway route as it heads southwest along Indiana State Route 2 from South Bend. After a couple of hours of quiet and

Lincoln Highway sign marking our precise route in Indiana

often quite scenic country driving in the early to mid-morning, traffic along the highway began to get notably more dense as we entered the huge Chicago metropolitan area, with its population of almost 10 million.

All of the Lincoln Highway alignments deliberately avoided Chicago itself. Even all the way back in 1913, it was abundantly clear that it was a poor idea to route a transcontinental highway through a city that was already well over two million strong. Of course, many early Lincoln Highway travelers temporarily left their path, heading along the various feeder roads described in the *Official Road Guide* to stay the night in exciting and cosmopolitan

The late morning drive from Matteson, Illinois to Dixon, Illinois

Chicago—at that time the second largest city in the United States and the sixth largest in the world.

Traveling Due West Just South of Chicago

Having made many stops in Chicago previously, we stayed on the highway and drove through the town of Merrillville (with a population of 35,000 the largest town in Indiana). Next came the towns of Schererville (passing Tiebel's Family Restaurant—open since 1929 and still going strong) and Dyer (home of another "Ideal Section"—this one about one and a half miles long). After crossing the border from Indiana into Illinois, we proceeded through the southern Chicago suburb of Chicago Heights, where we noticed a cool early Seventies Buick Electra 225 hardtop sedan waiting at an intersection. Ivelis and I are both big fans of the now almost entirely vanished hardtop body style—one without a B (or center) pillar.

Cool mild custom 1971 Buick Electra 225 sedan with *very* non-stock paint in Chicago Heights, Illinois

Shortly thereafter, the two of us stopped for a quick but tasty fast food breakfast in the village of Matteson (home of the 100 store Lincoln Mall). We headed almost due west through the village of New Lenox (where we first spotted one of the 36 handsome murals installed along the highway by the Illinois Lincoln Highway Heritage Coalition) and into the city of Joliet.

Joliet happens to be where the very first Dairy Queen opened back in 1940 (there are now more than 6,000 locations in 20 countries). The city also has a museum that I do believe that we might have enjoyed, but at the time we arrived it was open only for a particular bus tour group, but very explicitly *not* to two somewhat random folks traveling in a middle-aged Corvette. Moderately nonplussed by this state of affairs, I quickly took some unfortunately rather average photos of the intersection of the later Lincoln Highway route and our utterly *beloved* Route 66—which we have twice driven the entire length of and hope to complete again really soon. More than a little conscious of the need to keep moving along at an expeditious pace, Ivelis and I decided to get back in *Lauren* and drive on rather than waiting for the museum to open for us.

After leaving downtown Joliet, we drove in a northwesterly curve through the outer Chicago suburbs. In the large village of Plainfield, we passed a circa 1928 Standard Oil/Amoco gas station in red, white, and blue. Next came the city of Aurora, the birthplace of one of my favorite adventure novelists from back in the Eighties, Clive Cussler. Somewhere in Aurora, I made the mistake of believing the wrong road sign and turned due west just a few miles too soon onto the present-day US Route 30. Once again, the two of us quickly agreed not to backtrack, even though that meant we were going to miss the very first of the "Seedling Miles" in Malta. We proceeded on west through the village of Sugar Grove before fueling at a Shell in the small village of Big Rock.

Next, we continued through the villages of Hinckley (where the Harlem Globetrotters played their first road game in 1927), Waterman, and Shabbona. We turned just about due north on State Route 251 and rejoined the old highway in the small city of Rochelle (home of the notably railfan-friendly and engaging Rochelle Railroad Park). Next came the village of Ashton—things tend toward the small in this part of Illinois.

Visiting Franklin Grove

In the quiet village of Franklin Grove, about five miles southwest of Ashton, we stopped for a little over an hour in the early afternoon at the national

Entering small Franklin Grove, Illinois

headquarters of the relatively new but *very* active Lincoln Highway Association. Ivelis and I walked in and quietly signed the guest book. Already inside was another couple traveling the Lincoln Highway in what they told us was a far more leisurely fashion (measured in many months versus a few weeks) than ours. They were driving in an impressively well preserved and maintained (and evidently quite

Parked quite stylishly outside the national Lincoln Highway Association headquarters in little Franklin Grove, Illinois

functional) 1980s Volkswagen Vanagon Westfalia—I neglected to get the precise year.

An amiable woman named Lynn Asp (in general, folks were wonderfully gracious to us during this entire trip) spoke to us at length about the Association and their various upcoming events. It was only well after departing Franklin Grove that we realized that there is a picture of Lynn in one of the many Lincoln Highway-related books that we were carrying with us in *Lauren*'s rear compartment—we definitely should have gotten her to sign it!

After finishing our diverting and motivating visit to the Lincoln Highway Association's national headquarters, we walked across quiet Elm Street and ate a light and late lunch at the very cute and friendly **Lincoln Way Cafe**. There is a marvelous hand-painted map of the Lincoln Highway on one of their side walls, but I (sigh) neglected to take a photo (Ivelis would later claim that I was having too much fun). We finished eating and walked back across the quiet street to our parking spot. I worked myself into the driver's seat, dropped the power windows (it was getting rather warm), keyed the ignition, waited a few seconds for the sometimes balky fuel pump (another concern) to charge the fuel delivery system, and started *Lauren* without incident.

The Old Highway Reveals Itself

Beginning in this part of the route, Ivelis and I found that the existence of the Lincoln Highway as an authentic and still extremely present entity grows quite powerful and stays that way until well into California. Rarely does even a single mile pass without seeing some kind of highway marker—original, replica, or otherwise (the original Lincoln Highway Association considered it necessary that the highway was "A Well-Marked Road"). Businesses of all types also reference the highway; auto repair shops, bed and breakfasts, laundromats, restaurants, etc. The lasting power of Carl Graham Fisher's very effective branding from a century ago was quite evident. Of course, it was 2014, so the modern often intruded on our experience—as we headed west from the Chicago metropolitan area, we saw many recently installed wind farms dotting the landscape along our route.

Entering downtown Dixon, Illinois

After we departed from little Franklin Grove (population a little less than 1,000), next came the significantly larger city of Dixon (boyhood home of former President Ronald Reagan, who was in office when *Lauren* was new). Another 13 miles further along the highway came the city of Sterling, which among other features boasts a very cool-looking Art Moderne-influenced movie theater, whose design dates from 1944 and which has benefited from a recent and extensive renovation.

About fifty miles west of Franklin Grove, we stopped for a snack in the small city of Morrison, which is the location of another one of the early Lincoln Highway demonstration "seedling miles" —a short "Ideal Section" intended "to demonstrate the desirability of this permanent type of road construction." Several miles further west, we passed through the city of Fulton (named after steamboat

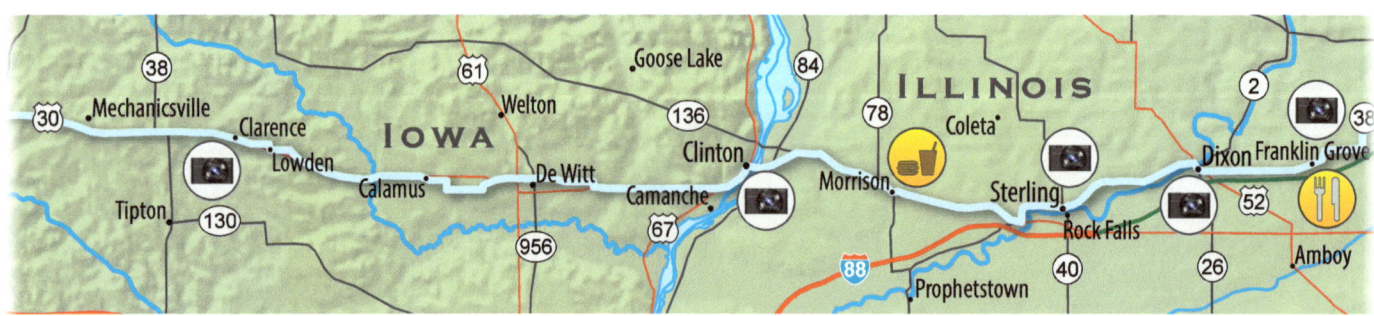
The early afternoon drive from Dixon, Iowa to Mechanicsville, Iowa

Cool theater marquee in Sterling, Illinois

1960 Ford F-series pickup truck marks one of Kinion Auto's locations in Clarence, Iowa

inventor Robert Fulton) and traveled across the circa 1958 Gateway Bridge while crossing the Mississippi River into Iowa at the city of Clinton, which designated itself as "The Crossing City" during the Lincoln Highway's early years. We rejoined US Route 30 in Clinton as we continued to follow the at least slightly more modern route.

again. We passed through the small city of DeWitt (named after politician DeWitt Clinton) and the very small city of Grand Mound (population 642). The town of Calamus (titled after the wetland plant prevalent in the area) was next as we stair-stepped back and forth across US Route 30. The very small city of Lowden followed—still home to the circa 1915 **Lincoln Hotel**, which is not only a bed and breakfast with five attractive rooms but also

Crossing the mighty Mississippi River into Clinton, Iowa

Just a bit after we had entered Iowa, we saw the older and newer Lincoln Highway routes merge yet

America, under construction —just west of Stanwood, Iowa

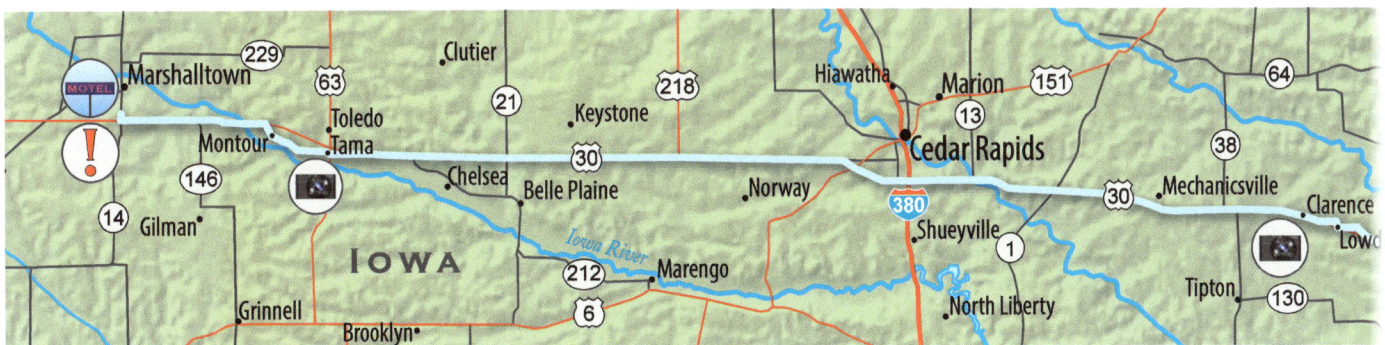
The early afternoon drive from Dixon, Iowa to Mechanicsville, Iowa

Warsaw, Indiana to North Platte, Nebraska

on the National Register of Historic Places. Next came the very small city of Clarence (population 974) where we met more highway construction that took us off our intended route for a few miles, and the small city of Mechanicsville. Only a few minutes later, we drove along just south of the relatively large city of Cedar Rapids—with a population of about 128,000, the 199th largest city in the United States.

King Tower Cafe on the outskirts of Tama, Iowa

Stopping for a Distinctive Bridge in Tama

Somewhat later on that same afternoon, we made it a point to stop at a charming little roadside park in the small city of Tama for a few minutes. We took some pictures of the very distinctive, quite cool, and oft-photographed hundred-year-old Lincoln Highway bridge, which was built with concrete.

Neat Lincoln Highway bridge dating from 1914 in Tama, Iowa

The bridge, which is on the National Register of Historic Places, was designed with the lettering on the railings in a largely successful attempt to make Tama stand out along the long cross-country route. Another view of the adjoining park is on this book's back cover.

After our short pause in Tama, the two of us passed relatively quickly through the tiny city of Montour (population 249) and the very small city of Le Grand (population 938). We stopped for the night in the city of Marshalltown. Among other things, Marshalltown is the birthplace of National Baseball Hall of Fame first baseman "Cap" Anson, who played in the late 1800s. In Marshalltown, Ivelis and I stayed at (you guessed it!) yet another national chain motel—the lack of any predictability in how far we would get each day had wreaked absolute havoc on our ability to stay in our standard preference for more unusual, historical, and distinctive places. We had traveled about 410 miles during the day and were now more than a thousand miles from home by the most direct and reasonable route.

Some Quite Frightening Weather

For much of that Tuesday afternoon, there had been various severe weather warnings popping up with alarming and steadily increasing regularity on both of our iPhones. These alerts matched the distinctly more foreboding skies we were driving toward. That evening we saw our first dangerous weather of this trip at about 7:30 PM, shortly after we had finished our dinner just across the street from the motel. There were multiple hail warnings, and we are acutely aware that hail and any kind of fiberglass do not get along! After all of this frightening build-up—I'll note that one feels much more vulnerable when significantly away from home—it finally did start to rain *extremely hard*.

In somewhat educated hindsight, we were quite lucky. Only 50 miles away from us, Story County reported quarter-sized hail at about the same time—and tornados are a significant risk in this area during this season. It did rain so profusely in Marshalltown that evening (about three-quarters of an inch)

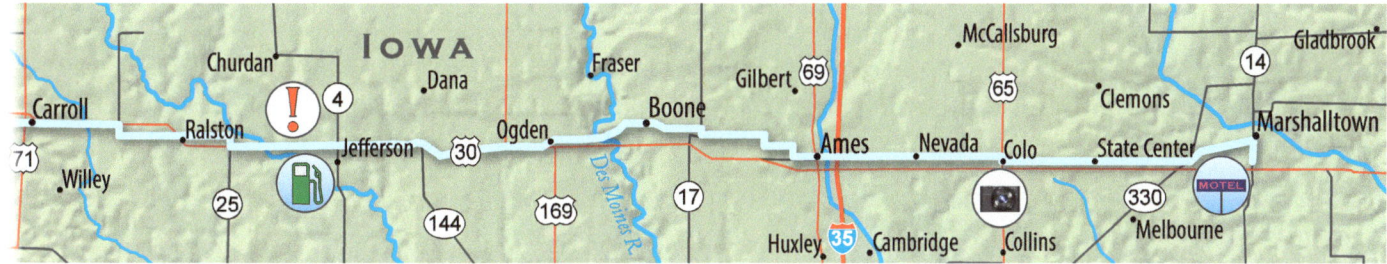
The early morning drive from Marshalltown, Iowa to Carroll, Iowa

that I became quite concerned about the possibility of significant amounts of water leaking past the original, aging, and aged weatherstrip around the targa top and side windows and into the passenger compartment.

At least in Marshalltown, that really heavy rain finally ended at a little after 9:00 PM. I quietly and very nervously left our motel room, walked carefully back outside, and checked on the car (Ivelis had, thankfully, done the smart thing and fallen quickly and comfortably fast asleep on the large motel bed). That original and correct weatherstrip that I had worried about so much had come through with flying colors; *Lauren*'s interior was as dry as a bone. This positive behavior was far from the only time on this trip when our aged "hooptie" surprised and impressed me in a positive manner. Ivelis corrects me on occasion by calling our 1985 the "*award-winning* hooptie …"

Returning to Normal?
The weather had fully returned to its senses by early the next morning (a Wednesday). The two of us ate a light breakfast and checked out of our motel. We wiped the remaining water off the car and left Marshalltown, heading just about due west. As the morning continued, we drove through the small city of State Center (a name reflecting its geographical location within Iowa) and the town of Colo (named after a railroad official's dog), with a gorgeous restored cafe, motel, and circa 1926 Standard Oil gas station.

Passing the lovingly restored Niland's Café and Colo Motel in Colo, Iowa

Next along our route came the cities of Nevada (which has held "Lincoln Highway Days" in August every year since 1983), Ames (where we passed what remains of the circa 1938 and long-closed Colonial Motel), and Boone (named after Colonel Nathan Boone, the son of explorer Daniel Boone). Afterward came the city of Ogden (named after a railroad official), the infinitesimal city of Beaver (population 48), and the city of Grand Junction (labeled as such because of being the junction of the now long gone Keokuk and Des Moines and the Chicago and Northwestern railroads).

In a sunny mid-morning, we fueled up at a Sinclair gas station (with that forever cool dinosaur logo) in the small city of Jefferson (first named New Jefferson and the birthplace of pioneering

Many scenic routes (in multiple directions) were available in Iowa

Warsaw, Indiana to North Platte, Nebraska

pollster George Gallup). Through absolutely no fault of its own, this particular Sinclair had no premium fuel available—they had only regular and plus at the pumps.

Old school gas station, car, and guy: John fueling *Lauren* at a Sinclair in Jefferson, Iowa

Of course, this turned out to be the point in the trip where we learned that *Lauren*'s *L98* engine (which has been utterly babied for the last decade) *really* wants premium—despite what the original owner's manual states. Until we were able to once again fill the tank with the preferred grade, there was significantly more engine knocking than usual under any amount of load and even a few (to me) hair-raising noises that sounded like real misses.

Despite the frightening drama coming from the engine compartment, Ivelis and I proceeded along past the city of Scranton (named for Joseph H. Scranton from Scranton, Pennsylvania), the tiny city of Ralston (named after the founder of the Bank of California), and the town of Glidden. We passed through the city of Carroll and the tiny city of Westside (population 299). Next came the four small cities of Denison, Dunlap, Woodbine (which features six blocks of restored brick highway originally dating from 1921), and Logan. Following that, we stopped in the small city of Missouri Valley for an early lunch.

Truss bridge carries the railroad over the Boyer River just west of Denison, Iowa

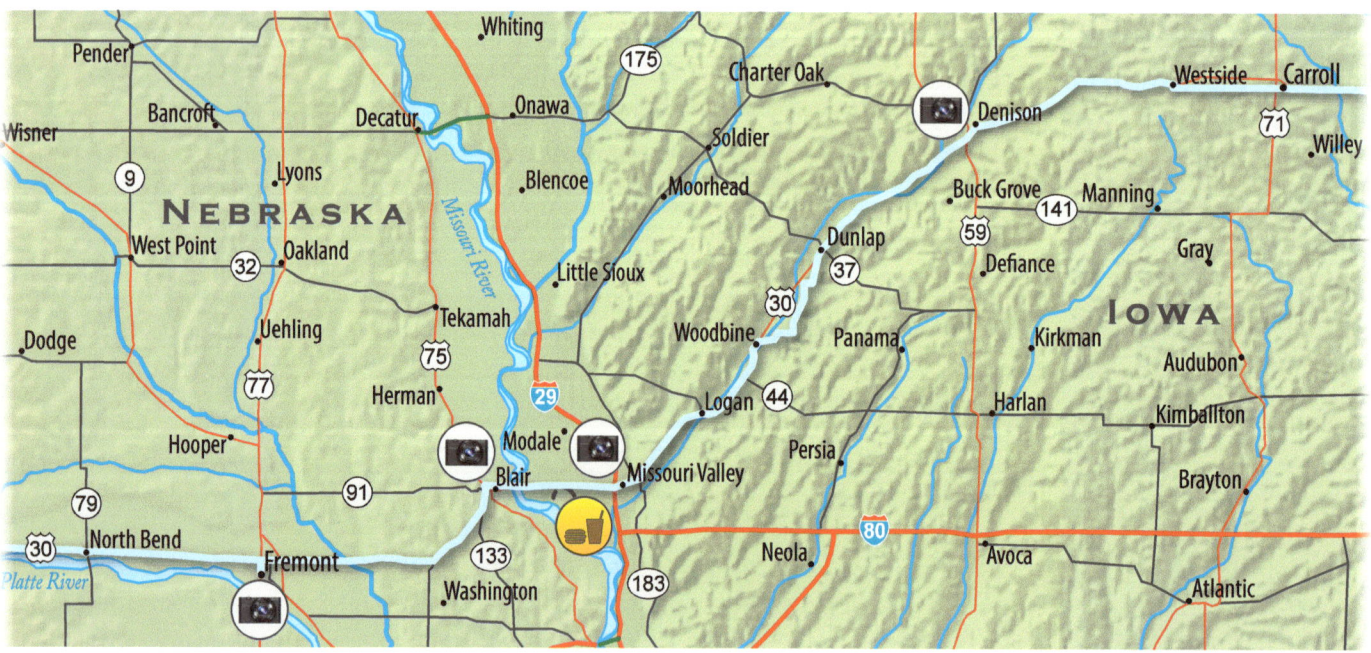

The mid morning drive from Carroll, Iowa to North Bend, Nebraska

Dairy Den ice cream and frozen yogurt shop (unfortunately not yet open for business when we passed it) in Missouri Valley, Iowa

Crossing the Missouri River into Nebraska near Blair

In Missouri Valley, our slightly newer route separated yet again from the original path. Ours headed due west while the older route headed due south toward Council Bluffs, Iowa and Omaha, Nebraska. We crossed the Missouri River, entering Nebraska about 25 miles north of Omaha in another small city named Blair (named for railroad magnate John Insley Blair).

Trains, Trains, and Yet More Trains

Ivelis and I both love trains, and that turned out to be a splendid thing on this trip. For the first two thousand miles or so of our journey west, railroad tracks were often within a few hundred feet of the Lincoln Highway. In many cases, this was a deliberate choice of the highway's planners, as the railroads had often done most of the hard routing (and blasting) work. The two of us saw many freight trains on those tracks, some with very unusual cargoes. At one point we saw a long train that included one flatcar transporting two M1 Abrams main battle tanks coming from the other direction. Both of us were too shocked by this sight to take a picture successfully.

Quite often, those very impressive freight trains we saw sported Union Pacific markings and insignia.

Long freight trains were our friendly and fairly constant companions for most of the trip

Warsaw, Indiana to North Platte, Nebraska

This turned out to make a lot of sense after I did some research. Even during our trip in 2014, a time when many folks believe that trains are supposedly almost entirely removed from the United States transportation network, Union Pacific alone still operates over 8,100 locomotives! That's definitely some food for thought …

Somewhere in the eastern part of the state of Nebraska, as we traveled near those seemingly endless train tracks, an engineer driving a long and heavily laden Union Pacific freight train heading toward us gave us a long and classic locomotive whistle merely for the fun and glory of it just after the two of us had both given him an enthusiastic wave. Ivelis and I both continue to believe that this was one of the coolest things that we experienced on our entire Lincoln Highway trip.

Some Positive and Negative Stops

Ivelis and I drove through the village of Arlington. Next, we parked in the center of the city of Fremont and took pictures of the statue of Abraham Lincoln (dedicated in 1921) in the quiet and pleasing **John C. Fremont City Park** (among other things, Fremont was one of the two first senators elected for the new

Statue of Lincoln in Fremont, Nebraska

state of California in 1850). After spending a few tranquil minutes holding hands as the two of us walked around the small park, we got back inside *Lauren*. We drove on along US Route 30 through the community of Ames (likely named after a Union Pacific official) and the small city of North Bend.

Next along our route came the small city of Schuyler. Ivelis has reminded me reasonably often since we finished this trip that I managed to get the only speeding ticket of our entire trip just to the east of Schuyler—and for no reason other than inattention (at least the deputy was polite). My only explanation (not an excuse) is this: as with most Corvettes, it is almost too easy to

The early afternoon drive from North Bend, Nebraska to Shelton, Nebraska

The Way Out, Part II

go fast in *Lauren*. In fact, like many of her predecessors from the Fifties, Sixties, and Seventies, she seems happiest at quicker speeds.

After that rather adverse stop (sigh!), next came the tiny village of Richland (population 73) and the city of Columbus (birthplace of Andrew Jackson Higgins, creator of the "Higgins boat" landing craft). In Columbus, we took a ninety-degree left turn and headed across the circa 1931 **Columbus Loup River Bridge** (on the National Register of Historic Places). Ivelis, *Lauren*, and I proceeded southwest on through the villages of Duncan, Silver Creek, and Clarks. We then drove towards the small city of Central City (named for its location within Nebraska's agricultural belt) and from there on to the city of Grand Island (birthplace of actor Henry Fonda).

In Grand Island (in 1936 the first city in the United States to install mercury vapor streetlights), we stopped for an afternoon snack, where the two of us shared a medium order of onion rings (ah, the glamor!) at a fast food restaurant. Grand Island is home to Nebraska's first "seedling mile," which

Remaining portion of the "seedling mile" in Grand Island, Nebraska

is well-celebrated—the Seedling Mile Elementary School (so named since the advent of the highway) is located along the original route. The City of Grand Island now owns the remaining visible 315 feet of that original mile, built in 1915.

After driving through the small city of Wood River, we stopped in the village of the Shelton to take some pictures outside Nebraska's Lincoln Highway Visitor's Center located between C Street and D Street. Unfortunately, the visitor's center had closed by the time we arrived, so we weren't able to talk to anyone from the Nebraska chapter. One of the photographs I took, with Ivelis once again waiting patiently inside *Lauren*, would become this book's front cover image.

It was now well into mid-afternoon and definitely starting to get warmer; up to about 80 degrees. Despite this heat, *Lauren*'s capable GM air conditioning was maintaining a comfortable temperature inside the car. This is especially impressive when you remember that we were traveling with the correct transparent targa top—an option chosen when *Lauren* was first ordered. We drove on through the small city of Gibbon. Long-time talk show host Dick Cavett believes that he was born in Gibbon, though this does not seem to be certain—the closest hospital at the time (1936) was in the city of Kearney, 17 miles further to the west along the Lincoln Highway.

Two Classic American Tourist Traps
We made a quick right turn just to the west of Kearney to take some very "touristy" pictures of

The late afternoon drive from Shelton, Nebraska to North Platte, Nebraska

Warsaw, Indiana to North Platte, Nebraska

Lauren with the famous and recently restored (the Lincoln Highway centennial was good to it) **Covered Wagon**, first built in 1932. The Covered Wagon was a symbol of the 1733 Ranch (once the home of what was claimed to be the largest barn in the world), so named because it was said to be 1,733 miles from both Boston and San Francisco.

Lauren parked next to the famous Covered Wagon just a little bit west of Kearney, Nebraska

After stopping at the Covered Wagon, we passed through the village of Overton and the city of Lexington, with its circa 1947 Hollingsworth Motel. Next came the small cities of Cozad (named after its founder) and Gothenburg (named after the second largest city in Sweden), and the villages of Brady and Maxwell. We stopped for the night at another relatively modern national chain motel in the city of North Platte, which started out in 1866 as a Union Pacific construction camp.

The motel we were staying in just happened to be located right next to yet another classic American tourist trap which has been far more consistently successful than the Covered Wagon we had stopped at earlier in the day: the **Fort Cody Trading Post**, which has somehow managed to stay in continuous operation for over fifty years. Ivelis enthusiastically took a bunch of pictures of the trading post as we walked past it, heading to a decent chain bar and grill for a relaxing and filling dinner.

Outside the Fort Cody Trading Post in North Platte, Nebraska

As almost everything on the route began to spread out a little more, our mileage per day continued to climb—we had traveled about 475 miles on this day. We were now about halfway through the Lincoln Highway portion of our trip without yet seeing any severe issues. However, Ivelis and I both sensed (it turned out correctly) that many challenges remained.

Hollingsworth Motel fades slowly away (note the dangling "H" in the red portion of the sign) on the highway in Lexington, Nebraska

The Way Out, Part III
North Platte, Nebraska to West Wendover, Nevada

The early morning drive from North Platte, Nebraska to Lodgepole, Nebraska

The next morning (a Thursday in late May) we woke up, showered, dressed, and packed bright and early. Next, Ivelis and I departed our comfortable motel in North Platte. Just before leaving, I took a careful look at our various analog and digital maps. Viewing them made me confident that Rock Springs, Wyoming was the only feasible stopping place within an approximately 210-mile range for our next day of travel along the Lincoln Highway. My best estimate was that we had about 500 miles of driving to reach our goal for the day.

Western Motel's sign reflecting on *Lauren*'s hood as we leave North Platte, Nebraska

Departing for Rock Springs

Less than a mile away from our motel, I fueled *Lauren* (luckily premium was available this time!) at another Sinclair gas station. We passed Scout's Rest Ranch (a palatial home once owned by William "Buffalo Bill" Cody) and some classic and engaging mid-century motels. Next, we drove just about due west on US Route 30 for about an hour through the villages of Hershey, Sutherland, and Paxton and the unincorporated community of Roscoe.

About 10 minutes west of Roscoe, Ivelis and I stopped in the downtown of the small city of Ogallala. In the 1870s, Ogallala was the terminus of the Great Western Cattle Trail; cattle drives that came almost 1,000 miles north from Texas. In Ogallala (named after a Sioux tribe), we posed *Lauren* in front of yet another restored gas station. I think I could comfortably create a full year's monthly calendar with the filling stations we photographed on this trip (six made it into this book). Afterward, we stopped just a few blocks away for a light breakfast and some pretty good coffee at the quietly welcoming **Lamp Stand** coffee shop.

Another beauty shot in front of another restored gas station—this one a Standard Oil Red Crown in Ogallala, Nebraska

After our relatively short pause in Ogallala, we pressed on through the village of Brule (named after the Brule Sioux tribe). Next, we passed the turn south for the Lincoln Highway's short-lived Colorado Loop which heads through the village of Big Springs on the way toward Denver. Instead,

Ivelis and I headed about 20 miles due west toward the very small city (population 929) of Chappell (named after another rail official).

Long Closed, but Yet Still Hanging Around

Shortly after driving through Chappell, we followed the advice of at least two of the many Lincoln Highway guidebooks we had packed and stopped mid-morning in the village of Lodgepole (population 318). After carefully driving a few blocks south of the Lincoln Highway onto what I remember as somewhat sketchy and almost entirely unpaved roads, we stopped for a couple of minutes and took some interesting and (perhaps?) evocative photos of *Lauren* parked in front of the **Lodgepole Opera House**.

Posing outside the long-closed Lodgepole Opera House

The Lodgepole Opera House was built in 1911 (when the village's population was closer to 500) and had its actual performance area above the garage. It closed in the late 1940s and was added to the National Register of Historic Places in 1988. It is more than a little bit surprising to me that the opera house is still standing after all these years and so many changes in purpose (many of them far from glamorous). Outside the opera house sat a well-used "Colonnade" Chevrolet Malibu Classic sedan (I believe a 1975) making *Lauren* look quite young in both years and (likely) mileage—what a difference a decade makes!

Unexpected Equipment Failure

I had definitely been expecting some issues on our trip with *Lauren*, but at some point, as we neared the Nebraska/Wyoming border, Ivelis reported an extremely unexpected problem from an entirely different source. On the list of issues we had not expected, my at that point still relatively new first-generation iPad mini had suddenly developed severe black banding that stretched across its entire 7.9-inch display—and the usual quick fixes (add/remove power, shut down/reboot) were not working. With its TomTom app (storing onboard maps of our entire route that did not require an internet connection) and its LTE connection (for routing around traffic issues), the mini had been serving quite capably as our primary digital navigation tool during this trip.

"We'll get it fixed at the nearest Apple Store," I said, quite confidently. Then (of course) we both discovered with the aid of our various other Apple devices that we were (doh!) manifestly not on either the east or the west coast where Apple Stores are quite prevalent. It quickly became evident that the next Apple Store anywhere near to our intended route along the Lincoln Highway was in Salt Lake City, about 550 miles to the west—or a little over a day of driving away.

Both Ivelis and I were more than a little nonplussed by this unexpected issue with our quite modern and (frankly) exquisitely over-maintained electronics. The two of us quickly switched to my iPhone 5 and its far smaller screen, which makes it notably sub-optimal for long distance navigation. Of course, the iPhone 5 also has nothing resembling the excellent battery life that any iPad has; relevant when one remembers that *Lauren*'s cigarette lighter hadn't functioned since before the beginning of our trip.

Details, Details, Details

The two of us drove on, with both the railroad tracks and parts of the 278-mile-long Lodgepole Creek quite close. We passed through the small city of Sidney—named after a railroad attorney and the

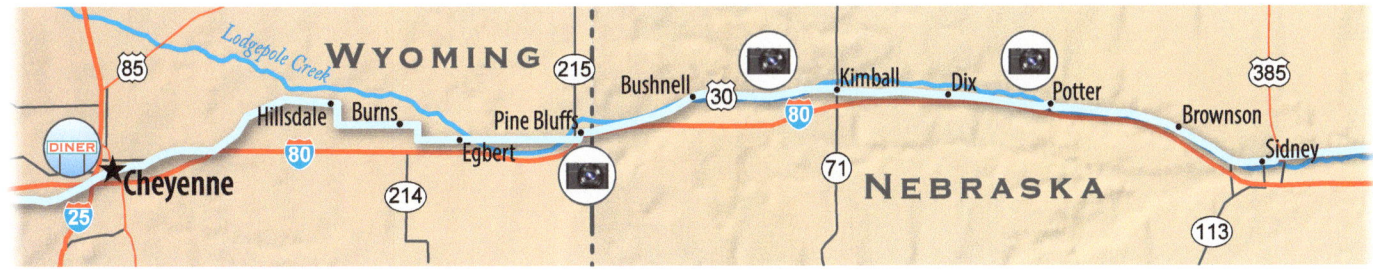
The mid-day drive from Sidney, Nebraska to Cheyenne, Wyoming

national headquarters of the Cabela's outdoor recreation stores. Next came the villages of Potter (featuring an interesting older Texaco station—there's a picture of it in the lists section of this book on page 67) and Dix, and then the small city of Kimball (named after a railroad official—sense a trend here?).

It is also often quite striking to see how carefully and attractively built some functional elements were around a hundred years ago. A few miles west past Kimball, we noted some well-maintained stone culverts under the still quite busy Union Pacific train tracks to our right. These contrast notably with the modern and (let's be honest) rather ugly ribbed steel versions you get quite used to seeing almost everywhere else as you drive along.

Entering Wyoming at Pine Bluffs

Nicely detailed stone culvert under the train tracks just west of Kimball, Nebraska

Ivelis and I drove through the village of Bushnell (named after Cornelius Scranton Bushnell—one of the people who spearheaded the development of the Union Navy's innovative *Monitor* ironclad warship during the American Civil War). Soon after, we crossed into Wyoming and the town of Pine Bluffs.

We headed almost due west, passing Egbert (probably best-known for being the location where the Union Pacific streamliner *City of Portland* was trapped during a spectacular and dangerous blizzard in January 1949), Burns, and Hillsdale. From there, the two of us headed slightly southwest, closing steadily on the center of the city of Cheyenne. Cheyenne is both the largest city in the state of Wyoming and also the state's capital—quick research indicates that combination as occurring in 16 of the 50 states in the union.

Visiting the Luxury Diner
As we arrived in downtown Cheyenne, I got only temporarily disoriented before successfully making a quick left turn across the busy traffic along the Lincoln Highway (locally labeled as Lincolnway) and stopping for lunch. Our stop for food was at an utterly great diner that most of our guidebooks had declared a "can't miss"—the **Luxury Diner**. This diner has been in existence since 1926; it is located near what is still a massive Union Pacific rail yard and depot (I counted at least 38 tracks and sidings).

North Platte, Nebraska to West Wendover, Nevada

Inside the trolley car portion of the rather excellent Luxury Diner in Cheyenne, Wyoming

We were quickly and efficiently seated all the way at the rear of the turn of the century trolley car that forms about half of the small eatery. Both of us perused the classically extensive diner menu carefully before ordering our meal. Shortly after that (service was quick, pleasant, and competent) I was enthusiastically consuming the green chili burger with cheese, which was both excellent and very filling—Ivelis pronounced that her bacon swiss burger was also exceptional.

The two of us felt quite refreshed after our enjoyable lunch in Cheyenne. We set out west-northwest on the Lincoln Highway towards the city of Laramie, following first State Route 225 and then Interstate 80. On the way to Laramie, Ivelis and I stopped for a few minutes at a brisk but quite striking overlook in Buford, quite near the highest point (8,640 feet) on the entire Lincoln Highway.

Lauren parked in rather threatening weather near the Lincoln Highway's highest point

This location on our trip also marks the point on the Lincoln Highway route where the "Transcontinental Touring" section of *A Complete Official Road Guide to the Lincoln Highway* gets notably grave with its "prospective tourists":

The lonely mid-afternoon drive from just west of Cheyenne, Wyoming to Sinclair, Wyoming

The Way Out, Part III

West of Cheyenne, Wyoming, always fill your tank at every point gasoline can be secured, no matter how little you have used from your previous supply. This costs nothing but a little time and it may save a lot of trouble.

Don't allow your canteen (west of Cheyenne, Wyo.) to be other than full of fresh water.

About 25 miles further northwest along our route, we followed that 90-year-old guide's advice, stopping to refuel *Lauren* at yet another Shell on 3rd Street in the downtown of the city of Laramie, named for French-Canadian trapper Jacques La Ramée. A little less than two miles north of our fuel stop along US Route 30, we drove slowly past the oft-photographed but now fading **Thunderbird Lodge**—advertised long ago as having "20 modern units." Ivelis' particular picture of the lodge resides in this book's annotated bibliography on page 69.

"Somewhere West of Laramie"

Laramie is the setting for the wonderful and historically significant "Somewhere West of Laramie" print advertisements for the Jordan Playboy two-seat roadster, first seen in *The Saturday Evening Post*. The founder and owner of the Jordan Motor Car Company, Edward S. "Ned" Jordan, wrote this immensely influential ad copy in 1923 at a point when the *Post* was the most widely circulated magazine in the United States. Many historians make the (I believe) legitimate claim that it permanently changed automobile advertising from being almost entirely about specifications and capabilities (economy, engine power, reliability, features, price, etc.) to being far more image-related.

Careful research indicates that Ned Jordan's use of Laramie as the particular location for his stunningly differentiating ad copy was at least semi-accidental. The phrase in the title of the advertisement was an off-hand comment by one of Jordan's traveling companions (we know he was a Mr. Austin) on a Union Pacific passenger train. That train was the famous *Overland Limited*, which at that time ran the 1,770 miles from Omaha to San Francisco in about two days. This was a 36 mile

per hour average speed which (of course) no vehicle driving on the early and often challenging Lincoln Highway could come close to matching.

Acknowledging these particular facets of American automotive history while we are traveling is relevant to me for various reasons—some of them not easily explained. I drove on for a little while until we were a few miles west (actually closer to north-northwest) of Laramie. The open land that Ned Jordan had written about all those years ago was visible around us, and those train tracks he mentioned were quite close.

We pulled over to the side of the highway somewhere near the unincorporated community of Bosler at a likely looking but also (of course) utterly unprotected location. I dashed across the road and took more than a few *once in a lifetime* pictures of Ivelis posing with *Lauren*. Conveniently, Ivelis' lovely long hair blew stylishly and appropriately in the wind.

Rain in Dry Wyoming

After that extraordinary photo opportunity (Ivelis is quite forbearing, isn't she?), we headed further west along some spectacularly empty and suddenly moderately wet roads. Wyoming is statistically quite dry throughout the year—only Nevada and Utah are drier in the United States. However, the two of us could see serious rain and strong thunderstorms off to our left and not so far in the distance.

With just a little bit of guidance from her owner, *Lauren* proceeded along in a remarkably

Thunderclouds and wet roads west of Laramie—notice that windshield wipers and headlights are both up

North Platte, Nebraska to West Wendover, Nevada

Somewhere West of Laramie

SOMEWHERE west of Laramie there's a broncho-busting, steer-roping girl who knows what I'm talking about.

She can tell what a sassy pony, that's a cross between greased lightning and the place where it hits, can do with eleven hundred pounds of steel and action when he's going high, wide and handsome.

The truth is—the Playboy was built for her.

Built for the lass whose face is brown with the sun when the day is done of revel and romp and race.

She loves the cross of the wild and the tame.

There's a savor of links about that car—of laughter and lilt and light—a hint of old loves—and saddle and quirt. It's a brawny thing—yet a graceful thing for the sweep o' the Avenue.

Step into the Playboy when the hour grows dull with things gone dead and stale.

Then start for the land of real living with the spirit of the lass who rides, lean and rangy, into the red horizon of a Wyoming twilight.

JORDAN
JORDAN MOTOR CAR COMPANY, Inc., Cleveland, Ohio

The original and magnificent Jordan advertisement from the June 23, 1923 edition of *The Saturday Evening Post*

THE SATURDAY EVENING POST   *May 23, 1985*

Somewhere West of Laramie

SOMEWHERE west of Laramie there's a broncho-busting, steer-roping girl who knows what I'm talking about.

She can tell what a sassy pony, that's a cross between greased lighting and the place where it hits, can do with thirty-two hundred pounds of fiberglass and steel and action when he's going high, wide and handsome.

The truth is—the Corvette was built for her.

Built for the lass whose face is brown with the sun when the day is done of revel and romp and race.

She loves the cross of the wild and the tame.

There's a savor of links about that car—of laughter and lilt and light—a hint of old loves—and saddle and quirt. It's a brawny thing—yet a graceful thing for the sweep o' the Avenue.

Step into the Corvette when the hour grows dull with things gone dead and stale.

Then start for the land of real living with the spirit of the lass who rides, lean and rangy, into the red horizon of a Wyoming twilight.

CHEVROLET MOTOR CAR COMPANY, Inc., Detroit, Michigan

My tribute completed in mid 2017, with the manufacturer, date, and description modified appropriately

North Platte, Nebraska to West Wendover, Nevada

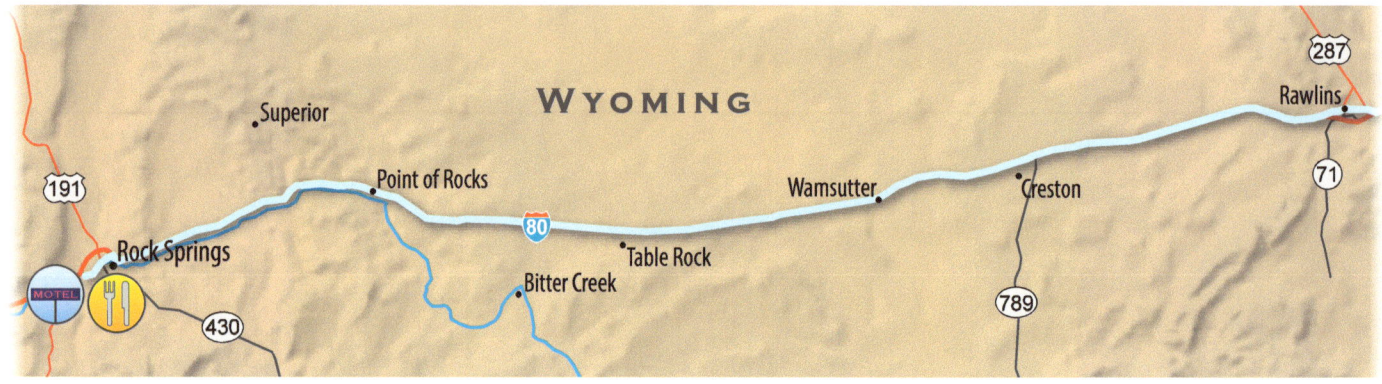
The late afternoon drive from Rawlins, Wyoming to Rock Springs, Wyoming

confidence-inspiring manner as if absolutely nothing was amiss, those snazzy rotating and retracting headlamps up and on, moving quickly, competently, and without complaint along the wet highway. She was not acting at all like a car that was almost thirty years old and getting some fairly fervent compliments from me.

Virginian Hotel in Medicine Bow, Wyoming

We continued through the small towns of first Rock River and then Medicine Bow, with its impressive 3½ story Virginian Hotel—circa 1911 and thus slightly predating the Lincoln Highway. This hotel comes out of absolutely nowhere and is completely unexpected in a town of only 284.

After traveling through Medicine Bow, we drove another 60 miles or so before rejoining Interstate 80 in Walcott, passing the town of Hanna along the way. We drove past the ghost town of Fort Steele (we saw more and more of these) and through the town of Sinclair (named after the energy company) on our way to the small city of Rawlins. Once through Rawlins (named after Union General and Grant administration Secretary of War John Aaron Rawlins), we drove on for about 110 reasonably quick and direct miles further west through the town of Wamsutter and the unincorporated community of Point of Rocks (population 3).

Late in the afternoon, the two of us stopped for the night at a relatively new and somewhat snazzy Holiday Inn in the city of Rock Springs. Ivelis and I finally took a deep breath, relaxed, and enjoyed a leisurely and surprisingly tasty dinner in the attached casual dining restaurant. On this day, we had traveled slightly over 500 miles in an aging *Lauren* along roads that were often both stunningly beautiful and chasteningly sparse. We were also now almost 2,000 miles from home and thus almost entirely detached from our regular support systems.

Toward a Potential Technology Fix

The next day was a Friday. In the early morning, we departed our relatively new and quite comfortable motel in Rock Springs. We fueled *Lauren*

Pausing outside Neldon's Custom Trim & Upholstery—an old and nicely repurposed Sinclair in Green River, Wyoming

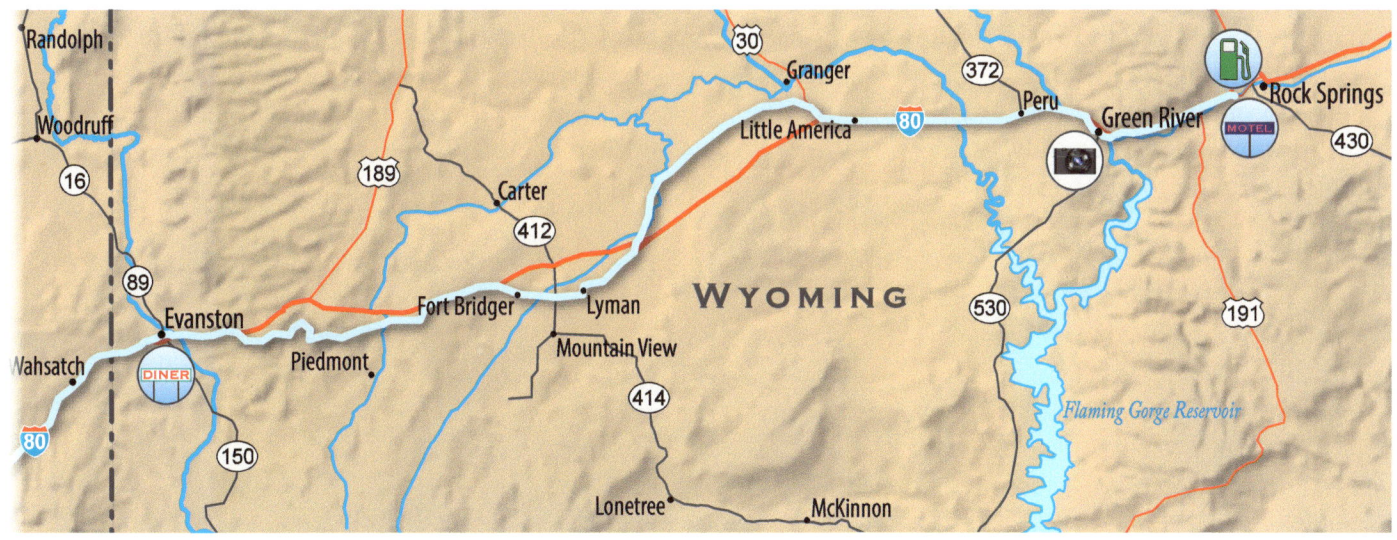

The early morning drive from Rock Springs, Wyoming through the ghost town of Wahsatch, Utah

with some more premium gas at a convenient local Mobil where we were situated across from a first-generation Porsche Cayenne SUV towing a trailer—not a typical sight back east! Ivelis and I headed west-southwest along the old highway toward the small city of Green River. In Green River, I couldn't help myself and stopped for some more beauty shots in front of an old, charming, and cleverly repurposed Sinclair gas station.

From Green River, we headed due west along Interstate 80; there's often no other viable option for road-bound vehicles traveling the Lincoln Highway at this point. Despite being on an interstate, the scenery was frequently gorgeous on this particular

America the Ridiculously Beautiful—on an interstate (!) on-ramp just west of Green River, Wyoming

morning in the middle of May. The two of us passed through the ghost town of Peru and the unincorporated community of Little America (named after the distinctive local hotel). Ivelis and I left US Route 30 for the last time after almost 2,000 miles a little to the south of the tiny town of Granger (population 139). Next, we headed southwest through Lyman and Fort Bridger (named after a nearby fort and trading post that opened in the 1850s) towards the city of Evanston.

At around 9:00 AM, Ivelis and I stopped for a quick but filling breakfast at **Jody's Diner** ("Where the locals meet and eat") on Bear River Drive in Evanston. Shortly after leaving Evanston, we crossed the state border from Wyoming into Utah. Not being very mindful of her age, I continued to push *Lauren* quite hard on through the ghost town of Wahsatch (last relevant in the 1860s), the small town of Emory, the tiny town of Echo (population 56), the small city of Coalville, and the town of Wanship. Next, we proceeded on west through Kimball Junction as we headed into the Salt Lake City metropolitan area and a hoped-for fix for our iPad mini in severe distress.

The late morning drive from Wahsatch, Utah to Salt Lake City, Utah

Downtown in Salt Lake City

Since neither Ivelis nor I had ever actually been in downtown Salt Lake City (I have "toe-touched" at the airport a few times), we ended up faithfully obeying our GPS navigation system. Not rewarding our faith, it took us on an extremely indirect and lengthy route (we passed through a few of the exact same locations more than once) to the very new (it opened on 2012) City Creek Center mall right in the middle of downtown Salt Lake City.

Lauren parked next to another very Eighties vehicle —a Jeep Grand Wagoneer

When we finally managed to make it to the mall, we placed ourselves in the underground parking next to a *very* Eighties Jeep Grand Wagoneer (dark blue paint with woodgrain side panels) in excellent repair—folks have been restoring these early SUVs for over a decade. Ivelis and I headed straight to the Apple Store, where I had scheduled a mid-morning appointment. The folks at this particular store were very competent: after we checked in and I described our issue, one of the Apple Geniuses looked at my iPad mini for about three minutes, verified my serial number, and told me that I was getting a brand new mini. Once we received our new iPad, it took about an hour or so for me to get just enough of our essential apps and services working to make both of us feel confident enough to leave the Apple Store and get back on the road.

We were already in downtown Salt Lake City and thus somewhat off our planned path—in fact, we were right on the earlier 1914 route which comes from north of the city. Ivelis and I decided to walk across South Temple (there's no street or avenue designation) to visit the 10 acre Temple Square. We viewed with interest it's spectacular and exceptionally well cared for Mormon buildings and gardens. This includes (of course) the imposing 7,000 seat **Mormon Tabernacle**, which began construction in 1864, was completed in 1867, and substantially refurbished between 2005 and 2007.

The mid-afternoon drive from just west of Salt Lake City, Utah to West Wendover, Nevada

Outside the Mormon Tabernacle in Salt Lake City, Utah

Returning to the Highway

After this unplanned and very brief tour of downtown Salt Lake City, we left the city and rejoined our later Lincoln Highway route. This course separates notably from the older routes for about 200 miles, initially heading due west instead of southwest—a significant part of the original highway in western Utah is now in the US Army's Dugway Proving Ground (which occupies 1,252 square miles) and thus entirely inaccessible. Just west of Salt Lake City, we stopped for a somewhat late fast food lunch in Tooele. The Great Salt Lake was to our right as we headed along Interstate 80 towards the Bonneville Salt Flats and Nevada.

We were unquestionably interested to see the Morton salt plant visible from the highway in Grantsville. After passing through Knolls, we were also—like I'll bet many an Interstate 80 traveler in Utah is—*completely nonplussed* by the 87-foot-tall "**Metaphor: The Tree of Utah**" sculpture just to the north of the highway as we neared Wendover. The tree was created under the supervision of Swedish architect, painter, and sculptor Karl Momen over a period of four years and dedicated in 1986. It has colored tiles on the six spheres attached to the trunk and deliberately "dropped" portions of spheres around the base. Strangely—or perhaps *not at all strangely* given this particular context—there is actually no legal and defined place to stop and take pictures of the tree.

Where at least some of that salt comes from; the Morton salt plant in Grantsville, Utah

Some things you just can't make up— "Metaphor: The Tree of Utah" in the western part of that state

North Platte, Nebraska to West Wendover, Nevada

Thus, Ivelis took our picture of "Metaphor" from inside a rapidly moving and thus notably vibrating *Lauren*—the speed limit on this part of Interstate 80 is (natch!) 80 mph.

One Item Removed From a Bucket List

Both of Ivelis and I had agreed quite early in our planning process for this trip that we positively wanted to visit the **Bonneville Salt Flats** in western Utah, something that has been on our automobile racing related "bucket list" for many years. If the salt is dry enough (and it isn't always so), the land speed record attempts happen every year in the middle of August (a streamliner with a twin-turbocharged small block Chevrolet V8 was clocked at *437 mph* in 2013). The rest of the year, the salt flats are a "special recreation management area" managed by the Department of the Interior.

Once we had passed the ghost town of Arinosa, we left Interstate 80 just east of the Nevada border and drove slowly out on a several-mile-long ribbon of asphalt. The speed limits are aggressively low—as if the civil engineers involved knew that there would be speed freaks driving along this road. The pavement ends in a kind of cul-de-sac, except there are (of course) no houses. What you do (if the salt is dry enough—and we were lucky that it was when we visited) is just gently drive off the asphalt and onto the actual salt flats.

the salt flats. Everyone present tried hard to avoid getting into each other's camera angles—I believe because all of us understood the flats' relevance. While Ivelis waited patiently, I spent about twenty to thirty minutes cleaning up *Lauren*'s exterior enough to make me comfortable with taking some (perhaps way too many) pictures.

You might not guess, but I am *extremely* happy in this picture

The eerie silence for the entire distance you can see and the absolute emptiness of the famous salt flats were both impressive and also striking—and not just for the beautiful pictures it produced, one of which is on this book's title page. Finally getting a chance to visit the Bonneville Salt Flats after so many years met both of our high expectations.

After taking our many pictures from various angles and then cleaning (the things you don't think of even when you get many hints!) a *lot* of salt off our shoes, we carefully drove back onto the asphalt and made a quick stop at the **Salt Flats Cafe** for refreshments. We stayed for the night only a few miles to the west, crossing just over the Nevada border to the small city of West Wendover. With all the stops on this day, both planned and otherwise, we had traveled about 330 miles.

We have arrived! Can you see the grit on the windshield?

There were six or seven other cars and trucks of various types (we spotted everything from minivans and crossovers to late-model Mustangs) on

The Way Out, Part IV
West Wendover, Nevada to San Francisco, California

The early morning drive from West Wendover, Nevada to just north of Ely, Nevada

Lonely and frighteningly beautiful US Route 93, heading south toward Ely, Nevada at about 7:10 AM

A**FTER STAYING THE** night right on the eastern Nevada border in West Wendover, we woke up quite early the next morning. This day happened to be the Saturday that begins the Memorial Day holiday weekend in the United States. Ivelis and I were hoping to cross the state of Nevada from northeast to southwest: a little over 450 miles—if, of course, nothing went wrong.

Early Morning in Northeastern Nevada

We showered, dressed, packed, and checked out a little before 7:00 AM. Next, the three of us fueled in the chilly (overnight, the temperature had dropped down to the low 50s) and quiet half-light at a Chevron gas station conveniently located just a few blocks from where we had stayed. While I filled *Lauren*'s capacious 20-gallon fuel tank all the way up, Ivelis cleaned the windshield. We also got some hot and decent coffee while we were at it.

We pulled away from the gas station, once again following the slightly more recent Lincoln Highway route. Leaving Interstate 80, Ivelis and I turned southwest along US Route 93A. We began our day by driving a little over one hundred very empty, quite lonely, but in their own way spectacularly beautiful miles.

Ivelis and I joined US Route 93 proper (known as "The Great Basin Highway" for unclear reasons) near the Stage Stop Bar-Cafe in the ghost town of Lages Station—you can see a picture of the intersection in the credits section of this book on page 76. About 20 miles further south-southwest, we rejoined the various older Lincoln Highway routes in the ghost town of Schellbourne. The two of us drove on both quickly and eagerly toward the small city of Ely and our appointment with the famous US Route 50.

Our first stop in quiet Ely was at yet another Chevron gas station to fill up with some more premium gasoline. Conscious of the need to keep

The eventful mid-morning drive from north of Ely, Nevada to just east of Austin, Nevada

the tank topped off, I fueled *Lauren*. Ivelis walked over to take a few pictures of some both interesting and also stylishly rusting old trucks that were a short distance away.

Old FWD truck rusting slowly away in Ely, Nevada

Absolute Carnage in Ely, Nevada

Immediately after we completed this quiet stop came *big and serious* trouble—the first with the car itself that we had seen on this trip. The carefully, expensively, and recently rebuilt passenger side door had been degrading steadily, becoming harder and harder to close over the first part of the trip. I had believed (or perhaps merely hoped) that it was just the new and tight seals, but Ivelis wasn't so sure. As we got ready to leave the Chevron, the door would not open at all from the outside.

After some rather desperate jiggling and jogging—I know a reasonable number of mechanical things about Corvettes, but I have a slight knowledge of or experience with troubleshooting or repairing aging Corvette doors—I finally managed to force the passenger door open from the inside. This basic result was a good one on the surface. However, one utterly unintended and especially frightening effect was that an approximately five-inch long steel part (the "outer door handle rod") ejected violently and almost vertically from the rear portion of the passenger door, nearly hitting Ivelis.

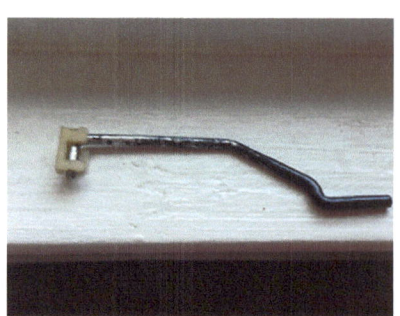
The part that ejected from the passenger door—the outer door handle rod with a small remnant of its clip attached

To make things worse, I tried to fix the lock and managed to make it so the passenger door wouldn't close. Making matters even worse, while trying to troubleshoot that lock, I generated the same result with the driver's side door.

At this point, I made a reasonably quick and painfully realistic assessment of our status. Ivelis and I were standing there, the two of us both highly perturbed Type As, next to an elderly and suddenly extremely questionable Corvette, neither of whose doors would close, in Ely, Nevada (almost 2,400 miles from home) on a Saturday morning during a holiday weekend. *Is this trip ending right here?*, I thought.

The next thing I did was something that I'll admit is quite uncharacteristic for me, but was unquestionably the right thing to do in this case. I "punted," walked slowly away from our degraded vehicle, went inside the Chevron, and asked the gas station attendant where the closest auto repair shop that was likely to be open was. He contemplated me for a few long seconds before telling me that the nearest mechanic was about five blocks further along Route 93 on the left.

We got back in our stricken (but still stylish!) Corvette. I drove *Lauren* quite slowly for those five blocks with both Ivelis and me somewhat desperately holding the car's long, heavy, and almost wholly non-functional doors as closed as possible.

Finding Help at Precision Auto Repair

Sometimes (I find fairly rarely) you get *extremely lucky* in your travels. The gas station attendant at the Chevron had given me helpful information and **Precision Auto Repair** was open and ready for business. Mike walked out of his garage bay as we pulled in and looked at our elderly car and the two of us a little quizzically. I carefully explained our problem(s), really hoping merely for some decent advice rather than a fix.

Precision Auto Repair sign in Ely, Nevada

Mike turned around and strode quickly back to one of his tool boxes inside the garage. He grabbed what remains to this day the largest screwdriver I have ever seen (I think it was a Snap-on). Then, he pulled the passenger side outer door handle up (doh!) and stabbed that enormous screwdriver deep inside. Paydirt! The passenger door closed properly (though it still didn't open from the outside). Mike walked around to the driver's side and did the same thing with it—and restored that door to absolutely full functionality. It had taken him all of *three minutes* to substantially fix our problems.

There was only one reasonable response we could give. "How much do we owe you?", I asked.

West Wendover, Nevada to San Francisco, California

"Nothing," said Mike, politely hinting that this was yet another somewhat stupid question from people who seemed to generate them with ease (and also strongly echoing the behavior of helpful folks in accounts of Lincoln Highway trips from a century ago). "At least give him a twenty," exclaimed Ivelis, and so that is what we did. I commented that we were definitely paying him a good hourly rate for his three minutes!

A Relaxed Breakfast Helps Decompress

We backed *Lauren* out from Precision Auto Repair's lot and got back on the Lincoln Highway, heading west once again. From this point, it was only a block west to our intersection with US Route 50, which we would be driving on for most of the day. With both of us feeling more than a little bit stressed out after all of this rather unexpected and yet much-dreaded drama with the car, Ivelis and I made a smart call. We drove only a mile further before stopping for breakfast—the second good decision we managed to make on that particular morning.

At about 9:00 AM, we paused for what I would characterize as a wonderfully calming (and also very filling—our waitress took good care of us) meal at the **24-Hour Café** located inside the authentically western-flavored **Hotel Nevada & Gambling Hall** situated in the center of downtown Ely.

Just outside the Hotel Nevada in Ely, Nevada

With 63 rooms and suites, the six-story-high Hotel Nevada has been in business since 1929. It was once actually the tallest completed and occupied structure in the entire state. This an honor currently owned by the massive fifty-floor/3,068 room The Palazzo casino hotel which opened in Las Vegas in 2007. Things have changed more than a little bit in Nevada over the last 80 years.

Antique racing poster inside the Hotel Nevada

For both Ivelis and I, an unexpected but very welcome attraction in that old hotel was the many fantastic auto racing-related posters from various eras attractively displayed throughout the first floor of the casino. We lingered in our comfortable booth in the cafe for much longer than we had remained for most breakfasts on this trip. Both of us were cognizant that we were now traveling with one more known problem in a somewhat wounded *Lauren*.

"The Loneliest Road in America"

US Route 50 in Nevada has been known by at least some as the "loneliest road in America" since *Life* magazine did an extensive and (to be honest) quite negative piece on the route with that title all the way back in July 1986 (when our *Lauren* was still a brand new car). One of the operative quotes from that rather brutal article (one has to wonder who on *Life*'s editorial staff had it in for Nevada) was:

> "'We warn all motorists not to drive there,' says the AAA rep, 'unless they're confident of their survival skills.'"

Like it says ...

In a common Nevada manner, the folks in this part of the state have made "lemonade from lemons." A potential visitor can actually (this is awesome!) send away to the Nevada Commission on Tourism for "The Official Highway 50 Survival Guide," which directs them to various points of interest along the route.

As we once again headed almost due west, Ivelis and I found US Route 50 to be at least slightly less lonely than some other parts of our route, such as US Route 30 west of Laramie, Wyoming and US Route 93 in Nevada. I am absolutely not stating that it wasn't lonely in many parts; on this particular Saturday, we often drove for 20 to 30 minutes straight without seeing even one other vehicle coming from the opposite direction.

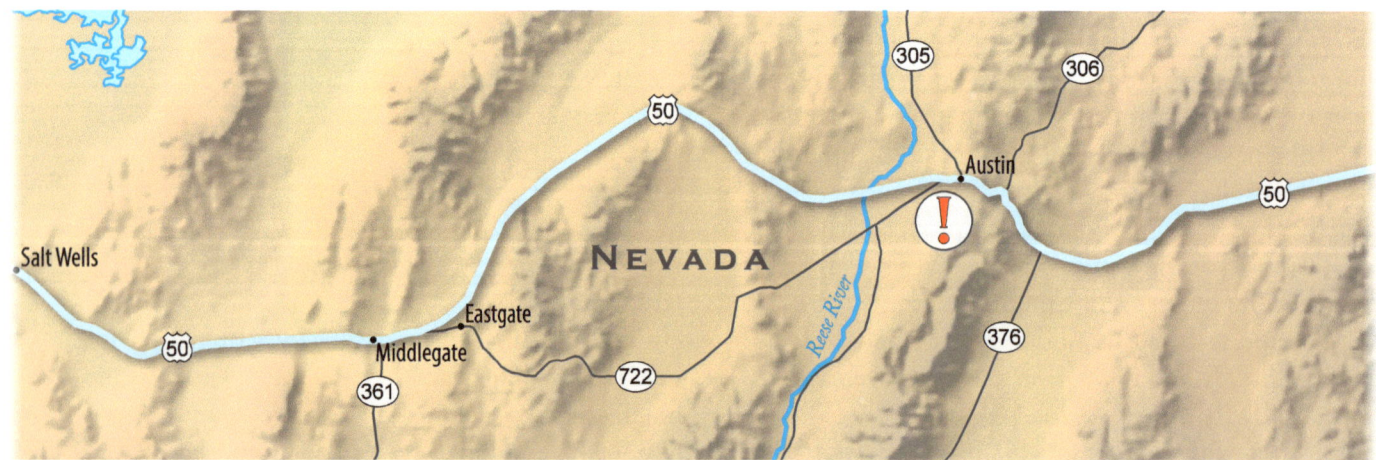

The mid-day drive from east of Austin, Nevada to Salt Wells, Nevada

The Way Out, Part IV

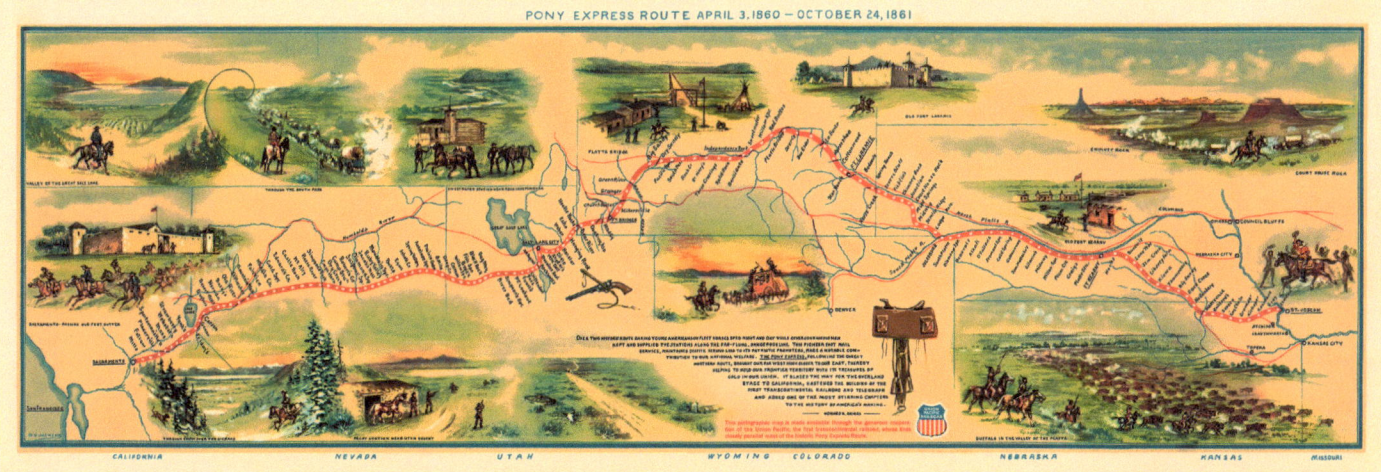
Gorgeous old map of the Pony Express route

Heading through one of the valleys on US Route 50

Austin is pretty confident

US Route 50 actually does seem less lonely and more just relatively endless at times: it crosses many broad desert valleys separated by numerous mountain ranges which tower over the valley floors. In this part of Nevada, the Lincoln Highway routes often parallel the path of the short-lived but very famous Pony Express mail service, which was in unprofitable operation from April 1860 to October 1861. We headed west on Route 50, passing through Eureka, which has a population of 610 and a lovely and recently restored circa-1880 opera house (a photograph is in this book's author's note on page vii).

Next came Austin (population 192), a silver rush town with billboards that state "What Happens In Austin … You Brag About." Heading west from Austin, we mistakenly stayed on the older Lincoln Highway route—taking the more modern one would have put us State Route 722 instead of Route 50.

Things became steadily less lonely as we headed further west along US Route 50, driving through Middlegate and Salt Wells. As we got to within about 25 miles of Fallon, we kept an eager eye out for the Loneliest Phone on the Loneliest Highway. At the time, we were perturbed at ourselves for somehow missing it, but I found out later that that particular pay phone was removed sometime in 2009.

F-5 Tiger II takes off from Naval Air Station Fallon in 2014

West Wendover, Nevada to San Francisco, California

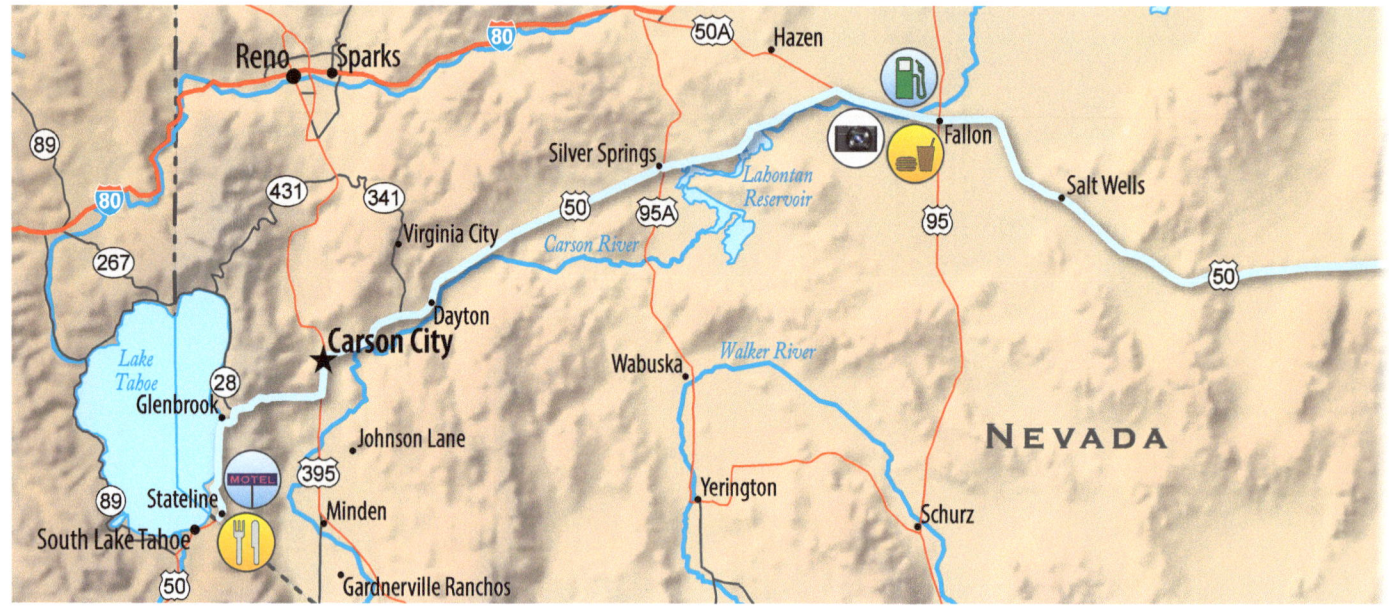
The mid-afternoon drive from Salt Wells, Nevada to Stateline, Nevada

In the early afternoon, we arrived in the small city of Fallon. Fallon is the current home of the **Naval Strike and Air Warfare Center**—the successor to the famous "Top Gun." While in Fallon, we fueled a hungry *Lauren* at a Texaco near Allen Road and ate a quick but filling fast food lunch at a Kentucky Fried Chicken about a block away. We managed to both decide on and also reserve our lodging for the night as we sat in a rather warm and quite sunny parking space outside that KFC. Afterward, we headed west from the center of Fallon, passing a commercialized static military aircraft display along the way.

Heading toward the circa 1931 Cave Rock Tunnel between Glenbrook, Nevada and Zephyr Cove, Nevada

Shortly after exiting Fallon, we separated yet again from the original Lincoln Highway route, turning southwest through Silver Springs and Dayton (the setting for John Huston's 1961 film *The Misfits*). We proceeded along the Carson River to Carson City (where Tour de France-winning cyclist Greg LeMond grew up). From there, we drove due south on very hilly roads—roads which challenged but did not defeat *Lauren*—through Glenbrook and Zephyr Cove with the exceptionally scenic Lake Tahoe visible immediately off to our right.

An Entertaining Night in Stateline

Early in that evening, the two of us arrived exhausted at the **Lakeside Inn and Casino** on

Cold War-era LTV A-7 Corsair II outside an auto dealership as we exit Fallon, Nevada

the Nevada side of the Nevada/California border in Stateline. In addition to experiencing that *brutal* morning issue back in Ely, we had driven about 465 tense miles.

Many modern vehicles are much bigger: *Lauren* absolutely dwarfed by a Ram pickup truck in Stateline, Nevada as night falls

The two of us unpacked and got somewhat settled in our room. Next, we headed out for an early dinner at the **Sage Room Steak House** in Harveys Casino—the scene of an utterly insane extortion plot and bombing all the way back in 1980. We had a delightful experience with three excellent waiters (Mark, Johnny, and Eddy), two of whom had been working at the Sage Room since the 1970s (!) and all of whom had their customer-facing routines well down. Ivelis and I had all of our dishes (except dessert) for two that evening—both the Caesar salad and the Chateaubriand were prepared tableside, and both were excellent.

That night Ivelis and I stayed comfortably and surprisingly peacefully at the Lakeside Inn. We had expected a lot more partying around us and our "standard" room's rather thin walls on a Saturday night during a long holiday weekend. However, both of us ended up getting a good night's sleep—perhaps because we were drained, possibly because the folks staying around us were pretty relaxed.

Of course, we got up early the following morning. After showering and dressing, I walked down the Lakeside Inn's exterior stairs toward our car. Taking advantage of the reasonably sheltered and easily accessible parking area, I opened *Lauren*'s large, heavy, distinctive, and expensive (insurance companies hated them—the primary reason that the next Corvette generation had a smaller and simpler version) clamshell hood, pulled the dipstick out, and checked the oil. It was showing just a bit low after almost 3,100 miles, so I added the quart of Mobile 1 full synthetic oil that we were carrying while we were still in the relatively protected parking lot of the Lakeside Inn. We had a little more than 200 miles left on our chosen Lincoln Highway route.

Our Excellent Small Camera Goes Missing

I couldn't tell you how, but we managed to lose our powerful, flexible, and capable but perhaps actually a little bit *too small* Sony Cyber-Shot DSC-RX100 camera somewhere in Stateline. We spent a couple of hours that morning in an entirely fruitless search of both the Lakeside Inn and the Sage Room. At this point, the two of us made the painful decision to give up, leave Stateline, and use our iPhones to take pictures for the rest of the trip.

Our little lost Sony RX100

After driving less than a mile, Ivelis and I crossed the border into California and South Lake Tahoe. The two of us headed along US Route 50 through the Echo Summit Pass (elevation 7,382 feet). We then drove a couple of hours' worth of spectacular and scenic winding roads through the Eldorado National Forest, passing through infinitesimal Twin Bridges (population 10), Kyburz (named for a postmaster), and Camino (home of many Christmas tree farms).

View while driving through the Eldorado National Forest near Kyburz, California

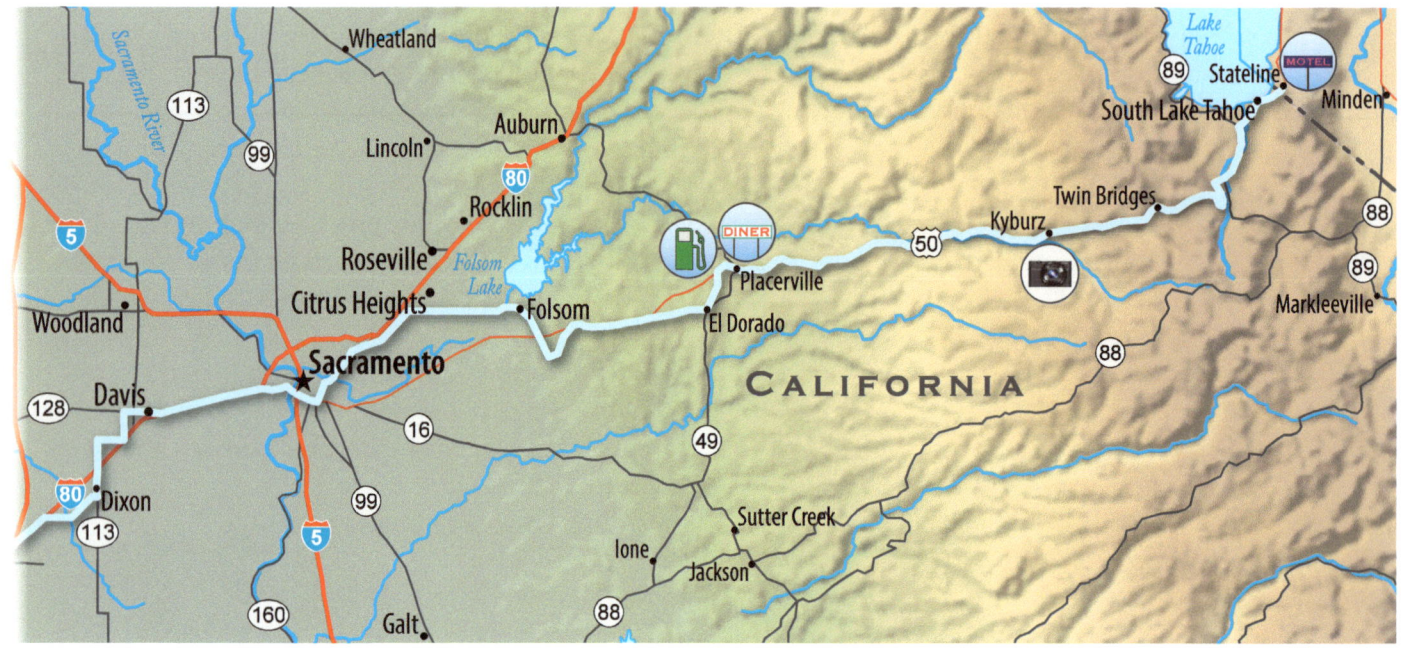
The morning drive from Stateline, Nevada to Dixon, California

Later in the morning, we stopped in the sunny city of Placerville (another Pony Express stop) for one more really good breakfast at **Original Mel's,** a fun retro-style diner inspired by the one in *American Graffiti*. We refueled at a nearby Shell with a little over a hundred miles left on the Lincoln Highway. After we had finished at that gas station's pumps, we parked right behind a gorgeous red 1965 big block Corvette Sting Ray convertible while we purchased some snacks and used the Shell's facilities.

As the morning continued into the afternoon, we drove on in increasingly heavy traffic (I could definitely feel us getting closer to the left coast) through the town of El Dorado and the city of Folsom. Next, we passed through the city of Citrus Heights and the state capital of Sacramento. At this point, we rejoined the earlier Lincoln Highway routes and (jumping on and off) Interstate 80. After that came the cities of Davis (named after a local farmer), Dixon, Vacaville (another Pony Express stop), Fairfield, and Vallejo.

More "social climbing"; parked behind a lovely "mid-year" Corvette in Placerville, California

A small map, but a *harrowing* afternoon drive from Dixon, California to San Francisco, California

Serious Problems in California Traffic
Shortly south of Vallejo, the Lincoln Highway becomes increasingly subsumed by much more

The Way Out, Part IV

modern roadways and, of course, the ferry from Berkeley to the Hyde Street Pier is long gone. Because of this, I made what turned out to be a flat-out dreadful decision to follow the advice of our GPS for the remaining part of the day's trip. We would likely have been better served by at least trying to approximate the original route through the Berkeley and Oakland area.

Despite (or perhaps because of) the fact that it was Memorial Day weekend, we ran into a ridiculous (but I'm told quite characteristic) traffic jam at the Interstate 580 on-ramp in Richmond, California. We moved no more than a quarter of a mile in an hour and a half.

I felt a certain sense of dread that there was trouble coming for *Lauren*—and for the second time in two days. Despite moderate ambient temperatures of around 70 degrees, there was precious little air coming through the radiator (because we weren't moving at all). I could see the engine coolant temperatures climbing steadily on the really snazzy for the mid-1980s driver information center.

I have to give the car at least some credit: *Lauren* somehow managed to hang in there for the first 45 minutes or so. She then vapor-locked (or something like it) as she overheated badly, causing wild engine surging and about five (*aaack!*) stalls, each one of them requiring an increasingly hard, lengthy, and painfully uncertain restart. This situation was positively *not* the relatively smooth and quick finish we had been hoping for. I suddenly had a very real, absolutely brutal, and quite visceral fear that, after making it 99% of the way out, we might not make it the final 25 miles to the Lincoln Highway's terminus.

However, once we managed to get through that particular ridiculous on-ramp and its associated toll booths, our travel was (stunningly) smooth sailing for the rest of the way into San Francisco. There was—almost unbelievably after the immediately previous insane traffic issues—hardly any traffic heading in our direction as we headed over the iconic **Golden Gate Bridge**. After that, it was a relatively straight shot down first Lincoln Boulevard and then El Camino Del Mar.

The Big Finish

We finally arrived at **Lincoln Park,** the western terminus of the Lincoln Highway, on May 25, 2014, at 3:50 PM. Interestingly, Lincoln Park was dedicated in 1909—a few years before the Lincoln Highway came into existence. It seems hard to overstate the power of the 16th president of the United States' name in the early 20th century.

According to the reasonably accurate trip odometer (it needed to be quite precise to pass an NCRS performance verification in June 2011), we had traveled a total of exactly 3,250 miles in nine days. Our Lincoln Highway portion had been about 3,150 miles in eight days or approximately 394 miles per day. The odometer also showed us averaging an absolutely astounding 26.0 mpg with that relatively large V8 and very rudimentary engine controls that were designed in the late 1970s. Still a little doubtful about this mileage, I confirmed the accuracy of the trip computer's numbers with our gas station receipts after our trip was complete—it turned out to be off by well under 1%.

Finally heading over the Golden Gate Bridge

Really bad photo, but that is exactly 3,250 miles on the trip odometer—no rounding. Note that coolant temperatures remain elevated following the "challenges" at the Interstate 580 on-ramp.

West Wendover, Nevada to San Francisco, California

Despite our painfully substantial delay, our friend Jordan was (still) patiently waiting for us at the circa 1924 **Legion of Honour** in Lincoln Park with very unexpected but excellent champagne and tasty cheese—undeniably taking a lot of the edge off what had been an extremely trying last day of our Lincoln Highway experience. He did seem quite perturbed that he had somehow

Marker at the Lincoln Highway's Western terminus

left some accompanying bread at his apartment, but we were certainly not complaining! The three of us spent a little more than an hour together eating, drinking, and talking on that breezy late afternoon. Afterward, we parted ways, with Jordan departing on his snazzy BMW R1100R motorcycle and the two of us driving a final five miles to our stop for the night.

Jordan welcoming us to the finish in style

The First Real Hotel Since Pittsburgh

We stayed in a "Grand Deluxe King Union Square View" room (O those hotel naming conventions) in the "Landmark" portion of the **Westin St. Francis**—a great bookend for our start all the way back at the Wardolf Astoria. The St. Francis is a lovely old (circa 1904) hotel on Powell Street, which somehow (perhaps the use of brand new materials and up-to-date construction techniques?) managed to survive the catastrophic 1906 earthquake reasonably intact. It overlooks Union Square, the absolute heart and soul (extra points for those who get the location appropriate Huey Lewis reference) of San Francisco. Our room on the 11th floor gave us an excellent view.

View of Union Square from our room at the St. Francis

Our "Wow, we actually made it!" celebration dinner was at **Michael Mina's Bourbon Steak**. I was exhausted and still more than a little stressed—my hands continued to shake for most of the evening. Thus, it was a good thing that this restaurant was conveniently located on the first floor of the St. Francis and not somewhere halfway across the city.

After Ivelis and I had eaten our excellent dinner, there was no further celebration that particular evening. We took the elevator right back up to our striking and comfortable room, turned in fairly quickly, and slept exceptionally soundly.

The Way Back, Part I
San Francisco, California to Denver, Colorado

The *long* first day heading back east—San Francisco, California to West Valley City, Utah

Usually, the trip back east from one of our transcontinental road trips is rather anticlimactic, but this was not the case this time around—we were mindful of *Lauren*'s multiple existing issues and the potential for some more. The two of us were also about 2,900 miles from home by the shortest reasonable route—and that wasn't nearly the one we were taking.

Starting Back East *Really Quickly*
It was quite early on a beautiful Memorial Day morning—I'm sure readers of this book are starting to get the idea that we were often on the road early in the day during this trip. Ivelis and I checked out of our room in the extremely stylish, very historic, and quite comfortable Westin St. Francis hotel in downtown San Francisco. In at least somewhat educated hindsight we had an *almost entirely unreasonable* goal of making it all the way to the Salt Lake City area on Memorial Day—a little over 750 miles, even with the reasonably direct and fairly quick route we were traveling. This distance was by far the furthest I had ever driven *Lauren* in a single day and was going to be a major challenge for us considering how challenging it can be to rack up serious miles in an early C4 Corvette.

With this context, I was definitely at least somewhat more keyed-up than usual as we pulled out onto Geary Street and took the quick left onto Mason Street. A few blocks further, we took another left on Eddy Street before angling right and following 5th Street southeast to the Interstate 80 on-ramp.

The two of us did get a splendid start on that particular morning. At least partially due to it being early in the morning on a national holiday, we actually managed to exit the San Francisco metropolitan area fairly quickly, heading out over a relatively un-crowded **San Francisco-Oakland Bay Bridge** on Interstate 80. This speed was an extremely marked contrast to our painfully slow and rather fraught entrance *into* the San Francisco area less than a day before.

With our path varying only a little from the Lincoln Highway route we had taken on the way into San Francisco, Ivelis and I quickly passed through the cities of Oakland, Vallejo, and Davis, along with the capital city of Sacramento. At this point, we separated from our later Lincoln Highway route and turned northeast through the city of Roseville (birthplace of iconic Eighties actress Molly Ringwald). Interestingly, we were now consistently within a few miles of the original Lincoln Highway route—the one we hadn't taken. With about 120 miles already on the road early in the day, we stopped mid-morning for a very filling breakfast at the amusing, clever, and welcoming **Black Bear Diner** in the city of Auburn (known because of its various fitness events as the "Endurance Capital of the World").

After refueling *Lauren* with some premium gas at a Shell conveniently only a few blocks away from our breakfast stop in Auburn, we drove on through the small city of Colfax (named for Schuyler Colfax, Ulysses S. Grant's Vice President) and the famous Donner Pass. Next came the city of Truckee and tiny Floristan (population 73). The three of us (don't forget *Lauren*) crossed the California-Nevada border near the tiny town of Verdi (population 162) and headed toward Reno.

Nearing the California-Nevada border in Floristan, California

A Relaxing Visit with Bill

Reno, with its population of about 223,000, is both the 90th largest city in the United States and (as they say there) "The Biggest Little City in the World," a phrase coined as the winning response to a $100 (!) contest back in 1929. We headed just a little bit off our route along Interstate 580 and some secondary roads toward the south of the city itself.

In the late morning, we stopped to visit with one of our good Corvette friends who we feel like we've "known" for years but had never actually met in person until this trip. Bill Hetzel is a longtime racing instructor—indeed, many aspiring racers in the Reno area swear by his skillset. He is also quite deeply into the process of restoring a 1967 "mid-year" Corvette Sting Ray coupe to better than new almost entirely by himself—what many of us who are participants in the restoration part of the Corvette hobby would think is a definition of absolute insanity.

Bill gave us a complete update on the current status of his restoration: it was really nice to talk about an old Corvette other than our 1985 for at least a little while. He also made me quite pleased by telling us that we had arrived significantly earlier in the day than he had been expecting us.

Back on the Road

After spending a couple of really relaxed, interesting, and motivating hours with Bill, we prepared to get back on our way to Salt Lake City. While we spent our usual couple of minutes getting ourselves situated inside the car, Bill took a few pictures of the two of us and *Lauren*. He posted them on the Internet shortly after that to confirm to folks following us on the various online Corvette forums that we are participants in that Ivelis and I were (at least) three things:

a) both alive
b) still traveling in a still at least somewhat functional *Lauren* (though Bill had both examined and commented on the *sordid* physical evidence of the passenger side door's disintegration)
c) as Bill stated in his forum post, "Spotted in Reno, headed east"

A few fun and relaxing hours spent with Bill in Reno, Nevada

Bill's photos independently confirm to the portion of the Internet that cares that we are alive and heading back east

The Way Back, Part I

After leaving Bill's house and departing the Reno area, we headed back out northeast along Interstate 80, passing through the rapidly growing and quite scenic city of Fernley before stopping for a rather quick lunch and some more fuel in the small city of Lovelock.

We then drove through the small city of Winnemucca and the city of Elko,

Between Reno, Neveda and Fernley, Nevada on Memorial Day

whose motto is "The Heart of Northeast Nevada." At this point, we were still just a little over halfway to our planned Salt Lake City stop for the night—and we were very definitely "burning daylight."

Lauren Makes it to 75,000 Miles
After driving through Halleck, we stopped again for gas at a busy and fairly modern Shell service station in the small city of Wells—you know that it is a long day's drive when you have already filled up the gas tank three times by the early afternoon. Shortly afterward, Ivelis somehow managed to get a good picture of *Lauren*'s odometer with her iPhone in a notably vibrating vehicle (Interstate 80

Turning over 75,000 miles —thanks, Ivelis!

often isn't at all smooth in Nevada) at speed as it turned over to precisely 75,000 miles.

We finally crossed the border into Utah near Wendover, rejoining what had been our Lincoln Highway route on the way out west for a little over a hundred miles. Shortly after that, we passed

San Francisco, California to Denver, Colorado

a car driven by some people who had not followed the often repeated advice to not just randomly drive onto the generic salt flats along Interstate 80. They had, of course, gotten stuck in the wet salt— I'm willing to bet that the locals in the area make a pretty good business towing folks who haven't listened to the warnings out.

As we had expected, it was a *very* long day's drive, but we neared the Salt Lake City metropolitan area just as darkness began to fall. We managed to negotiate one final stretch of highway construction—a good thing as I felt my reaction times starting to fade. I had driven *Lauren* about 765 miles in a single day; a fairly impressive number even in a much newer car.

Just off Interstate 215, the hotel we arrived at in the West Valley City suburb south of Salt Lake City was brand new (you could smell the fresh paint) and quite nice. However, the hotel restaurant that I had planned for us to eat dinner at was closed because it was Memorial Day (doh!). Hungry, thirsty, and *really* drained, we made a snap decision and walked a couple of blocks east over to a fairly new TGI Fridays in the nearby Valley Fair Mall. At that Fridays, we had a decent and filling meal, good drinks, and a skilled and funny waitress—just the ticket after such a long day on the road.

One Final Bonus on Memorial Day
Finally, there was one more unconditionally excellent bonus for us on this particular long, eventful, and rather amazing Memorial Day. After eating dinner, the two of us walked back to our hotel and began our regular nightly process while traveling of getting our clothes out of our luggage for the next day. While doing so, Ivelis found the little Sony RX100 camera we thought we had lost two days and almost a thousand miles prior, all the way back in Stateline, Nevada. After a short celebration which was mostly composed of the two of us dancing around our hotel room, we happily went to sleep.

After we woke up, showered, dressed, and packed the next morning, we had a pleasant breakfast at our hotel before getting back on the road. We headed southeast towards Denver (about 525 miles away), taking Interstate 15 south through the cities of Lehi, Orem, and Provo before switching over to US Route 6 in the city

Our route from West Valley City, Utah to Denver, Colorado

of Spanish Fork (the first Icelandic settlement in the United States). We drove along through and Helper, stopping in the small city of Price to fill up at a Chevron and passing through Wellington before Route 6 joined Interstate 70 near the tiny city of Green River (population 973).

Heading southeast on Route 6 in Utah

The Right Roads for *Lauren*

Ivelis and I shared a glorious revelation on our way back home. On smooth and either newly paved or very well maintained roads at 75 mph or so, *Lauren* became absolutely silent except for wind noise: you could not hear the tires or the engine—though I could still feel some of the throb of the *L98* engine making its way through the chassis and the gas pedal. In addition, there were none of the usual creaks and rattles expected in an early C4. After ten years of ownership, we had finally found a few perfect roads for *Lauren*.

Obviously, these were the kind of roads that the Corvette Chief Engineer in *Lauren*'s time (David McLellan) had in mind when he and others designed the car for all those years ago in the late Seventies and early Eighties. I mentioned this to Ivelis as we moved along and all she had for me was a "Wow!" — it was so completely outside of our usual experience when driving this car.

Of course, the good often comes with the bad: we also discovered the limits of that at one time very "hi-tech" *Driver Information System* trip computer in our 1985 Corvette—the trip odometer can only count to 4,096 miles (almost certainly due to an absolute memory limitation in the internal computer). When we went over that magical number, the trip computer suddenly *lost its mind*, giving us ridiculous mileage and range values. Luckily, a single push of the reset button in the center console made that problem go away—I wish everything with *Lauren*'s often rather sketchy electronics were such an easy fix!

Entering Colorado From the West

In the early afternoon, we crossed the state border into Colorado about 10 miles west of the tiny unincorporated community of Mack—there's not a lot that exists right on the Utah-Colorado border near Interstate 70. About ten miles further east from Mack, we paused for a quick break at the very pleasant and welcoming Colorado Visitor's Center in

Interesting Western Slope
Vietnam War Memorial in Fruita, Colorado

Leaving Utah for Colorado

Fruita (free coffee!). The visitor's center adjoins the impressive Western Slope Vietnam War Memorial, with its real UH-1H "Huey" helicopter, forever either taking off or landing—depending on how you view these things.

Just a few miles and a couple of minutes further down the road, Ivelis and I stopped at for a late lunch at another modern and quiet McDonald's in the city of Grand Junction as we continued to make our way through the Rocky Mountains. After eating, we stopped for gas at a Shell in the town of Parachute before proceeding through the small city of Glenwood Springs and the famous ski town of Vail.

We then drove through the **Eisenhower–Johnson Memorial Tunnel**—built starting in 1968 and ending in 1979 and, at 11,158 feet (over two miles) above sea level, both one of the highest vehicular tunnels in the world and the highest point in the entire 46,876-mile Interstate system. Even when the two of us passed through in late May, there was still a significant amount of snow in the area, and it was more than a little chilly.

Cool modified mid 1960s Chevrolet pickup truck frames *Lauren* in Grand Junction, Colorado

Nearing the Eisenhower Tunnel—snow!

San Francisco, California to Denver, Colorado

Down Some Horsepower at Altitude

Though she had been running quite well in general for the previous day and a half, *Lauren* was unmistakably beginning to show some signs of loss of horsepower because of the altitude. This condition was not at all unexpected—at 11,000 feet above sea level we were probably down at least 75 bhp from the *L98*'s factory rated 230 bhp (a rating my almost thirty-year-old car probably doesn't achieve under the best of conditions). I managed to compensate at least somewhat by continuing to aggressively bump the automatic transmission down to a lower gear, which kept the engine RPMs up. However, Ivelis and I were certainly both concerned with the striking loss of performance.

After a few more hours up in the mountains, the two of us passed through the small city of Idaho Springs. From that point, the interstate descended fairly rapidly towards Denver, dropping more than halfway back to sea level and allowing our aging engine to regain a good portion of its horsepower.

Denver, Always Wonderful

I had promised Ivelis before we began this trip that on the way back home we would do our best to stay in quite nice and very comfortable hotels in the middle of major cities and now it was time to come through on that promise. The first of those hotels was the sleek, modern, and comfortable **Westin Denver Downtown** on Lawrence Street in Denver's wonderful and walkable downtown—by coincidence (no planning here!) only about two blocks northeast of the route of the Lincoln Highway's Colorado Loop.

We were in Denver for dinner on my actual birthday. That dinner was at what I already knew (from a previous solo visit) was the marvelous **Elway's Downtown** steakhouse in The Ritz-Carlton on Curtis Street. Elway's is not like many other restaurants associated with retired sports stars. Part of the sell—and it is an effective one—is that it is the kind of place that John Elway himself (the Hall of Fame and Super Bowl-winning quarterback) likes to go to, and they execute on that concept very well. In particular, I found that their

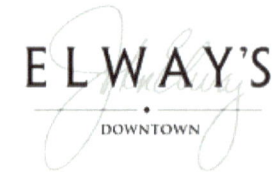

shrimp cocktail delivered with dry ice (with three sauces—cocktail sauce, remoulade, and Joe's mustard sauce) was the best and most interesting version of that dish that I had ever had.

Spectacular looking and amazingly good shrimp cocktail at Elway's in Denver

Ivelis had "spilled the beans" and confirmed to the staff that the birthday we were celebrating was mine. As a final thoughtful touch, one of our two excellent waiters at Elway's sent us off with a tin of their steak seasoning, which we have definitely enjoyed. Afterward, we walked back to our comfortable Westin for a nightcap and some quiet and relaxed sleep. After two very positively eventful days, we were now about 1,700 miles from home.

Unusual and really nice birthday touch —a tin of Elway's Steak Seasoning to go

The Way Back, Part II
Denver, Colorado to Indianapolis, Indiana

Our (mostly flat) route from Denver, Colorado to Kansas City, Missouri

The next morning we woke up refreshed and ready to get moving quickly on another lovely late May morning—I have found over decades that Denver mornings throughout the year are often sparklingly attractive. After showering, getting dressed, and repacking, the two of us checked out of our extremely comfortable hotel. We drove a few blocks south to take several pictures around downtown Denver. Both Ivelis and I took many photos of the imposing and distinctive 40-foot tall fiberglass and alloy steel **Big Blue Bear** statue formally titled as "I See What You Mean." Local artist Lawrence Argent's bear is forever peering perhaps quizzically inside the glass wall of the Colorado Convention Center on 14th Street. For an unexpected reason, that huge bear is accidentally blue—an early drawing that was supposed to be sandstone in color came back from the printers in blue instead, and Argent evidently took that as an inspiration. Would that my many color correction issues became so artistic!

Big Blue Bear staring into the Colorado Convention Center

""Go" Discovered in the Hills" mural in downtown Denver

Leaving Denver Fairly Slowly

After our admittedly short but quite enjoyable visit to the central business district (some Denverites abbreviate it as CBD) neighborhood of downtown Denver, we got back in *Lauren* and took the Colfax Avenue on-ramp onto Interstate 25 North. After only a few miles, we headed east along Interstate 70 with an eye to making it to Kansas City by evening—a little over 600 miles of what the two of us hoped would be relatively easy and low-stress highway driving. We made solid morning progress; Ivelis and I had a quick fast food breakfast in the town of Bennett and filled up

55

Lauren's 20-gallon gas tank at a Phillips 66 in the small city of Burlington.

Entering Kansas—note that it is not *quite* as flat as the cliche

Gorgeous and iconic "Bandit" Trans Am actually being driven in Kansas

We crossed into Kansas near the small city of Goodland and headed through the small cities of Oakley and WaKeeney (that name is a rather strange combination of Warren and Keeney). Afterward, we drove through the city of Hays and stopped in the city of Salina, where we filled up yet again at a Shell and ate yet another fast food lunch. While we were stopped, I gave *Lauren*'s hard-working *L98* engine another quart of motor oil—this time (in honor of her mileage now being over 75,000) using some Quaker State High Mileage.

There Are Clearly Other Cool Cars

The two of us saw many cool cars of all kinds on this trip, but one particular vehicle stood out for Ivelis and me from of all of the others. This automobile was an iconic black and gold 1978 "Bandit" Pontiac Firebird Trans Am coupe (with a long CB antenna sticking out from the center of that ridiculously small trunk, of course) driving east on Interstate 70 on the way to Junction City. As we rapidly closed on it, we could see that this particular Trans Am was a superb restoration—nearly perfect and unquestionably much nicer than it was when it originally was built in either the Norwood, Ohio or the Van Nuys, California assembly plants (both of which have been closed for decades).

You so rarely see these second-generation Firebirds and Camaros out on the road now (even less are now being driven than our early C4 Corvettes) despite the fact that they were immensely popular in their day. General Motors produced over three million "F-bodies" between the 1970 and 1981 model years. Almost half a million of those were Pontiac's top-of-the-line (and not at all inexpensive—this 1978 was a minimum of $7,058—about $28,600 in 2018 dollars) Trans Ams; Burt Reynolds really should have gotten at least a small commission on each of them after filming *Smokey and the Bandit*. The relatively few ones that remain and weren't entirely beat to heck have been getting notably more valuable recently; all of them are now at least 37 years old. Ivelis gave the woman driving the Trans Am a great big wave as we passed in the fast lane. I puzzle over if she wondered if she should know who we were?

After passing through Junction City, we drove on through the cities of Topeka and Lawrence in the late afternoon as we neared the Kansas City metropolitan area. We took the Kansas Turnpike for most of the final portion of our day and crossed over the Kansas River into Missouri on Interstate 670.

Downtown Kansas City Astonishes

Once in Kansas City, we stayed in the Crown Center area at another Westin hotel. This hotel both overlooks and adjoins the spectacular circa 1926 **Liberty Memorial** that commemorates World War I

Entering downtown Kansas City on Interstate 670

Outside the magnificent Union Station in Kansas City

(a highly-rated museum is also part of the complex). The Liberty Memorial is across Pershing Road (named after the general in the Liberty Memorial) from the lovely and beautifully restored circa 1914 **Union Station** (I learned while researching this book that "union" at that time meant that multiple railroad companies stopped at the same station). It's also not far from the triangular **Western Auto Building**, originally built for the CocaCola Company in 1914 and now the home of stylish loft condominiums. Hopefully, the reader gets the idea by now that downtown Kansas City has many *very* picturesque portions.

A little over half an hour after we had checked in to the hotel that evening, Ivelis and I walked about ⅔ of a mile to **Fiorella's Jack Stack Barbecue**

A small portion of the Liberty Memorial in Kansas City. In order from left to right, that's Admiral Beatty (UK), Marshall Foch (France), General Pershing (USA), General Diaz (Italy), and General Jacques (Belgium).

Denver, Colorado to Indianapolis, Indiana

in the recently hip Freight House area. Jack Stack has been a going concern since their original storefront barbecue opened all the way back in 1957 on Prospect Avenue in south Kansas City. Both of us consumed substantial portions of many different kinds of delicious barbecue before walking quite slowly back to our hotel for the night. We'll surely return to Jack Stack if we get a chance (and I found out later that those evil folks also do mail order). I will admit that the two of us did stop at the charming Brasserie in the lobby of our hotel for a final and enjoyable cocktail before heading back to our room.

Circa 1914 Western Auto building in Kansas City

Heading Toward Indy

The next morning, we departed our distinctive, comfortable, and cavernous (at 450 square feet about ¼ the size of our entire house) "Park Corner" room on the 11th floor of the Westin in downtown Kansas City and checked out of the hotel. As we prepared to leave, we received a substantial amount of positive reinforcement from the hotel's parking valets—I believe that most valets on this trip thought that the two of us were more than a little crazy but also perhaps worth rooting for. We were certainly not driving a car they would see every day.

After Ivelis and I had left the hotel, I dealt with just a little of Kansas City's early to mid-morning rush hour contention along Interstate 670 before returning to the now very familiar Interstate 70, heading east. The two of us drove on towards this day's destination: Indianapolis—"only" about 485 miles away.

We stopped for a quick breakfast and some more fuel in the small city of Concordia. No matter how unexpectedly good the fuel mileage you are getting on a cross-country trip, there's still a lot of filling up when you are in an almost thirty-year-old car with a digital fuel gauge that is notoriously (frighteningly?) inaccurate as the gas tank gets within 25% of empty. Afterward, we continued driving almost due east past the cities of Columbia and St. Charles.

Around mid-day, we drove through the St. Louis metropolitan area in a rain that faded somewhat annoyingly back and forth between light and medium strength, some notably heavy traffic, and a lot of highway construction. Shortly after that, we crossed back over the mighty Mississippi River on the Stan Musial Veterans Memorial Bridge into Illinois and began to head in a slightly more northerly direction toward Indianapolis.

Searching for a Sonic

One of our many rather silly or strange objectives for this trip was that we hoped to stop for lunch at a **Sonic** drive-in at some point—but we had yet to be able to find one when we were ready to eat. The Sonic name dates from 1959 (they originated in Oklahoma) and they're

Kansas City, Missouri to Indianapolis, Indiana

The Way Back, Part II

Back in Illinois, with a bird perched on top of the sign

great fun though rather high in calories. With only a few days remaining, I was getting a little worried that this was one supposedly easy goal (there are over 3,500 Sonic locations in 44 states) that we actually wouldn't be able to check off on this trip. We finally found a well-timed Sonic along our route in the small city of Vandalia. After we exited the highway and stopped, we promptly ordered the obvious chili cheese dogs.

At last! We finally stop at a Sonic drive-in in small Vandalia, Illinois

After our successful Sonic stop, we drove through the city of Effingham, home of Mid America Motorworks, which has done an excellent business of supplying us with many of *Lauren*'s replacement parts over the last ten years. The owner of Mid America, Mike Yager, also owns the MY Garage Museum, which is a relatively small but spectacular collection of Corvettes and air-cooled Volkswagens (the other portion of the Mid America business), full of rare and unique cars. The two of us had previously visited the museum in mid-2008, so we did not make a stop on this particular trip. Ivelis and I did stop for gas at a Phillips 66 in the small city of Casey in the middle of the afternoon.

America, still under construction; entering Indiana

Next, we crossed into Indiana near the city of Terre Haute (original home of the Overland Automobile Company) as we closed in on Indianapolis along Interstate 70. The three of us only left the interstate when we were less than two miles from our destination for the evening.

Not all glamorous driving on the way back—
rain (some of it in focus) and
construction (out of focus) in western Indiana

Impressive Indianapolis

Every time we have stayed for a night, Indianapolis has been quite good to the two of us, and it was once again on this particular trip. This time, we overnighted right downtown at the Sheraton Indianapolis City Centre. Ivelis and I had stayed in the same building when it was a Radisson (hotel locations do seem to change branding often, don't they?) on one of our "big trips" almost a decade prior.

Denver, Colorado to Indianapolis, Indiana

The magnificent Soldiers and Sailors monument in downtown Indianapolis

would be a relatively straight shot over familiar territory—if, of course, nothing else went wrong with the car.

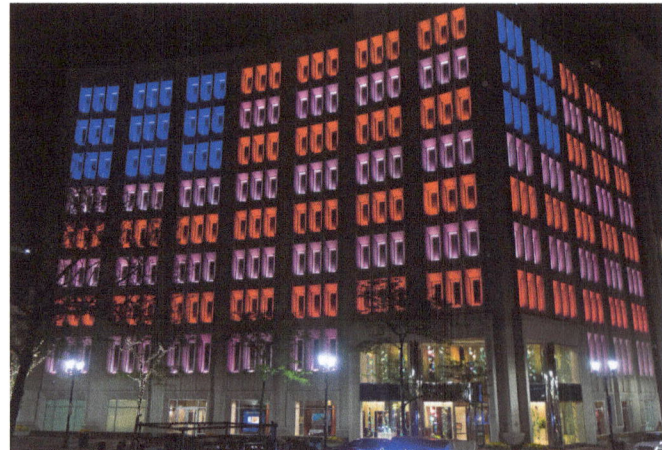

Indianapolis Power & Light Company's building on Monument Circle in downtown Indianapolis

After we checked in and got settled into our 11th-floor room, Ivelis and I freshened up and headed out on the town. The two of us (of course) re-visited the wonderful and magnificent **Soldiers and Sailors** monument in the absolute center of the city (dedicated in 1902 and on the National Register of Historic Places). After taking some pictures, we walked a few blocks over to our now traditional for Indianapolis dinner at **Ruth's Chris Steak House**. The reason for that dining choice is a long story from another trip almost ten years ago …

Ivelis and I strode around the pleasant downtown of Indianapolis for a while longer after dinner. We stopped for one more drink at the second Capital Grille of the trip before returning to our hotel room for a satisfying night's sleep.

After traveling for four days and about 2,385 miles in a somewhat indirect but fascinating route from San Francisco to Indianapolis we found ourselves a little over 660 miles from home. From here, it

The Way Back, Part III
Indianapolis, Indiania to Bryn Mawr, Pennsylvania

Indianapolis, Indiana to Columbus, Ohio

Ivelis catching me suddenly very serious (and not at all ready for a photograph) next to Dan Wheldon's final Indy 500 winning car

The next morning (Friday), Ivelis and I woke up, packed, and checked out of the Sheraton in downtown Indianapolis. We then drove about six miles in the opposite direction from our general route home, heading northwest to visit the **Indianapolis Motor Speedway** complex, which is in the town of Speedway. Originally envisioned by the same Carl Graham Fisher who worked so hard to make the Lincoln Highway a notable success, the Speedway has been holding races since 1909 and is on The National Register of Historic Places. Late in every May, the Speedway hosts 200,000 or more spectators for the Indianapolis 500, making it one of the largest single-day sporting events on earth.

The First of Two Great Museums

We spent a little over an hour in the Speedway's amazing **Hall of Fame Museum**, with its expansive collection of Indianapolis 500 racecars (along with some other interesting and impressive cars of various types) displayed in 30,000 square feet. It was wonderful to see so many of the winning Indy 500 racecars from my youth from all those drivers that I hold in so much esteem (Foyt, Unser, Rutherford, Johncock, Sneva, and Meers).

I'll freely admit to several exceptionally sobering minutes when I realized that I was standing right next to Dan Wheldon's Indianapolis 500 winning car from May 2011. Dan (a short but incandescent racing driver born in Emberton, England) would die only five months after this, his second Indy 500 victory, in a thoroughly horrifying and (the worst part) *completely unnecessary* crash at the Las Vegas Motor Speedway—auto racing so often takes its best and brightest.

After visiting the museum, Ivelis and I took what the Speedway calls the Grounds Tour. Traveling in a small bus, we visited much of the massive (it spans 559 acres!) Indianapolis Motor Speedway complex in a little over ninety minutes. Our stops included the iconic and many times rebuilt and enhanced "pagoda" timing and scoring tower (there's a picture in this book's index on page 73), the massive media center which can accommodate 1,000 press members, the paddock, and the track surface itself.

Ivelis sitting in the middle of the huge Indy media center

The particular tour group we were part of that morning seemed to be generally composed of perfectly nice folks who had been told (correctly) by someone they trusted that this was the most interesting place to visit in the Indianapolis area, as opposed to completely "wack" motorsports crazies like Ivelis and me. Suffice it to say that we were very definitely the first people in our tour group to take pictures of each other kissing the famous yard of bricks at the start and finish line on the front straightway—though many joined in once they got the idea. Kissing the bricks is a relatively new but now quite well accepted Indy tradition begun in 1996 by one of our favorite racing drivers, the long-retired Dale Jarrett, who is now in the NASCAR Hall of Fame.

Ivelis kissing that very famous yard of bricks at Indy

After our wonderful time at the Indianapolis Motor Speedway (I definitely have to get Ivelis back there for an actual Indy 500 race within the next several years), we headed east along 16th Street for a few miles, merged onto Interstate 65 South, and returned to Interstate 70 East. Now moving considerably closer to home, we stopped for lunch in Greenfield and proceeded through the city of Richmond (birthplace of noted composer Ned Rorem) before crossing the state line into Ohio, and heading toward the city of Dayton and a very different museum from our previous visit.

Another Amazing Museum

The **National Museum of the United States Air Force** is located at the large (almost 12 square miles in size) Wright-Patterson Air Force Base just east of the Dayton city limits. The museum was absolutely spectacular—perhaps even more interesting than the Hall of Fame Museum we had seen that same morning back in Speedway. When compared to, say, the also excellent **Smithsonian Air & Space Museum** in Washington, DC, which has a collection of somewhat similar size, the museum has the differentiator of concentrating perhaps 90% of its collection of approximately 360 aircraft, spacecraft, and missiles on (of course!) the United States Air Force.

A 2011 aerial view of the very impressive National Museum of the United States Air Force

The National Museum of the United States Air Force has many aircraft on display that even I—with a reasonably significant amount of air and space interest and knowledge—had never even actually seen in real life, much less seen up as close as we could at the museum. The museum also has the space available to display multiple versions of historically important aircraft such as the McDonnell Douglas F-4 Phantom II, which was in Air Force service for over thirty years (from 1964 to 1996). Ivelis and I continued to enthusiastically tour the museum until it was just about to close for the day and we both believe it was time very well spent.

Very early wooden wind tunnel at the National Museum of the United States Air Force

I had never actually *seen* a Convair B-58 before this!

Walking in Columbus

After leaving the museum and Dayton itself, we drove northeast, got back on Interstate 70 East, and

Now a museum—a wonderful old fire house in downtown Columbus, Ohio

drove past the city of Springfield, heading towards Columbus. That evening, we stayed in the almost brand new Hilton Columbus Downtown in Columbus' Arena District. After getting settled in our comfortable and rather high-tech room, we walked a scenic but somewhat circuitous (we'd never stayed in downtown Columbus before and it showed) half-mile or so to **Mitchell's Steakhouse** on 3rd Street, located in a spectacular old bank building, for yet another excellent dinner. I noted with some pride that we'd been doing pretty well for dining as we headed back east.

After dinner, we walked a significantly more direct route back to our hotel, passing the world headquarters of Nationwide Insurance and stopping for one last drink at our hotel's quiet and welcoming Gallerie Bar.

One Final Day on the Road

Early the next morning, we left our hotel in downtown Columbus, both of us knowing that, barring a severe mechanical failure (still a definite possibility), we would be back home in Bryn Mawr that night—we had "only" about 460 miles to go. We drove down 3rd Street taking an on-ramp onto Interstate 70. Just a few miles east of Columbus on the highway, we fueled *Lauren* at a Shell in the city of Pataskala and drove through the city of Zanesville, traveling a route that has become familiar to us during our various road trips.

We crossed the Ohio River into West Virginia at the city of Wheeling (birthplace of Pittsburgh Pirates' Hall of Fame second baseman Bill Mazeroski—he didn't have to play ball very far from home). Just as it had been on our way out, we were in the state of West Virginia for a rather short period (just a little under 15 miles) before crossing into Pennsylvania near West Alexander.

We drove our most eastern portion of Interstate 70 (we had been on I-70 for almost

The final day—Columbus, Ohio to Bryn Mawr, Pennsylvania

Indianapolis, Indiania to Bryn Mawr, Pennsylvania

West Virginia flashing by quickly once again

1,800 miles and about four days) before it joined the Pennsylvania Turnpike in the borough of New Stanton, home of a major UPS hub. Shortly after getting on the Turnpike, we made our last fill-up of the trip at the Shell located at the South Somerset rest stop.

A Brand New Corvette Motivates

As we headed closer to home on what to the two of us is a very familiar turnpike, we rather quickly approached and passed an extremely bright Torch Red C7 Stingray (the absolute "latest and greatest" Corvette and one that I and others think has at least a passing styling resemblance to our C4) near the borough of Carlisle, where the mind-blowing *Corvettes at Carlisle* show has been held every August for over 30 years. As we passed them, both C7 occupants (whose car has about twice the horsepower that our car has and is infinitely more technically advanced) gave us an enthusiastic and traditional "Corvette wave." Ivelis and I both viewed this as a great final omen (we were still looking for them even on this last day out) for this trip.

The final miles of our journey passed fairly quickly, as we proceeded along in very pleasant weather and at least somewhat rational turnpike traffic (it was a Saturday). We drove past Harrisburg, Hershey, and Lancaster, before exiting onto comfortable and well known to us local roads at King of Prussia.

Final mileage—77,427 and change

Ivelis and I arrived home safely but quite spent at our house in Bryn Mawr on May 31, 2014, at roughly 3:40 PM. We had traveled approximately 6,314 miles, and we had (amazingly) *made it* in our 29 and a half-year-old car. I felt like both we and *Lauren* should have received some kind of medal!

Coming up quickly on a very cool and brand new Corvette Stingray near Carlisle, Pennsylvania

The road takes its toll—about eight days of bugs

Afterword

A Few Conclusions

The three of us had been on the road for a total of 15 days. One day was spent "staging" to Times Square, New York City, eight traveling from Times Square to Lincoln Park, San Francisco on the Lincoln Highway, and six returning home (actually five and a half because we stopped for significant amounts of time at those two amazing museums on our second to last day out). I have to give credit to the weather in mid to late May of 2014—for the most part, it was near perfect. So many of our photos of this trip include beautiful blue skies.

For all of my worries and concerns about our ability to successfully complete this trip in this car, we ended up having only two major issues—the passenger door and the stalls. For the final eight days of our journey, I remained quite concerned that the passenger door would disintegrate even further than it had in Ely, Nevada. However, Ivelis and I were able to use both the manual door lock and the inside door handle all the way back home. Despite these problems, I'm very glad that we took this excursion in *Lauren*—I think that this choice of vehicle made the experience more special.

Perhaps we should have sensed this, but cross country travel on the Lincoln Highway turned out to be sharply different in feel from traveling Route 66. I think part of this is because of the previously mentioned "Route 66-industrial complex," but I think part is also because Route 66 is also much newer—the final portions of the "Mother Road" were decommissioned in October 1984, only a month before *Lauren* was built.

What I also know from experience is that time will deepen and change these impressions and conclusions. As I complete this second edition in mid 2018, I believe that the lasting memories will be as good as the initial ones.

Some of What's Happened Since the Trip

A few days after our trip was complete, Ivelis casually informed me that her request for a list of Chevrolet dealers situated along our route was *not* for a set of good repair locations, but rather so we could purchase a brand new C7 Corvette if *Lauren* suffered some catastrophic mechanical failure. "I brought my checkbook!" she stated rather forcefully. No wonder poor old *Lauren* managed to make it!

On top of this particular nugget, Ivelis also told me that she saw me more consistently happy during this trip than she has ever seen me before.

In June 2014, we drove *Lauren* to a wonderful local show run by the very competent *Boardwalk Corvettes* club in Smithville, New Jersey. Though we didn't win any major awards, we did receive many enthusiastic compliments for actually driving our aging car for such a long distance.

That same month, we got *Lauren*'s stricken passenger side door fixed. The quote from one of the mechanics involved when he saw the offending part was "that never breaks!"

On November 16, 2014, *Lauren* turned precisely thirty years old. We celebrated her birthday by taking her for a medium-length Sunday afternoon drive, visiting a TGI Fridays (an appropriately 1980s-era) restaurant in Exton, Pennsylvania along the way, which closed a bookend from that unexpected Memorial Day dinner back in West Valley City, Utah.

Lauren at (precisely) thirty

The Lincoln Mall in Matteson, Illinois closed in January 2015 after 41 years in operation, showing that even the Lincoln name can't protect from all the vicissitudes of change.

In April 2015, the original Palm restaurant at 837 Second Avenue in New York closed for major renovations. Things evidently didn't go nearly as planned and it never reopened—another part of the older (circa 1926) New York City departed. I'm quite happy we were able to have dinner there and see all those famous caricatures before they disappeared forever.

Also in April 2015, an extremely powerful *EF4* tornado hit Franklin Grove and Ashton on the Lincoln Highway in Illinois. Amazingly, only two people were killed.

Quick selfie taken outside the original Palm restaurant —now gone forever

Again in April 2015, we were traveling across country (again!) in a much more modern (27 years newer) Corvette. This very different vehicle did not stop one of the parking valets at the Westin Kansas City from recognizing us. "Weren't you here in an older blue Corvette last year?" he said. My experience continues to be that just when you don't expect folks to remember you (how many different cars and people does a valet see in a year?) is when they actually do.

In August 2015, the world's oldest Goodyear dealership in Lancaster, Pennsylvania was sold after remaining in the same family since 1854.

World's oldest Goodyear dealership was sold after 161 years with the same family

In the middle of September 2015, we had a 200-mile jaunt planned in *Lauren* (we had been invited to show her at the lovely and historic Ephrata Cloister). Only 15 miles into the trip, *Lauren* completely keeled over in the town of Malvern, Pennsylvania—the fuel pump that was original to the car had failed at about 78,000 miles and 31 years. Why it made it through our entire Lincoln Highway trip, I'll never know—but I am grateful that it did. Perhaps our somewhat astounding fuel mileage on the journey could be attributed to the fact that the fuel pump was giving the engine a little less fuel than it was designed to!

Michael Mina's Bourbon Steak at the Westin St. Francis in San Francisco closed in March 2016, though he still has many other restaurants in operation.

Also in March 2016, the aluminum Regional Enterprise Tower in Pittsburgh began renting apartments—that has got to be a cool place to live.

In June 2016, the National Museum of the United States Air Force in Dayton, Ohio added a fourth huge hall. This gallery displays an additional 70 aircraft, including the Boeing VC-137C (based on the 707 jet airliner) that served as the primary Air Force One transport from 1962 to 1972.

During our annual visit to *Corvettes at Carlisle* in August 2016, I was able to have *Lauren*'s exterior designer, Jerry Palmer, autograph two posters. He seemed impressed that I had brought something so personal to be signed—both posters were of *Lauren*, one taken on the Bonneville Salt Flats.

In September 2016, the Lincoln Highway Association sent us the *Bernie Queneau Coast-to-Coast Lincoln Highway Recognition Award*, which certifies that we have driven the entire length of the Lincoln Highway. Bernie was one of four Eagle Scouts who (along with three scout leaders) traveled the entire Lincoln Highway in July and August 1928 along the same route we would take 86 years later. He passed at the age of *102* in December 2014.

As I completed this book, I noticed the similarities between my grandfather posing with his Alfa Romeo and me posing with *Lauren* on the Bonneville Salt Flats. I am almost certain I did *not* see that old photo before we took our Lincoln Highway trip.

And, because the two of us are who we are, Ivelis and I began planning for another long journey in a Corvette …

Lists

Cassette Tapes in the Center Console

The functional and era-appropriate cassette tapes that we carried in *Lauren*'s cassette tape holder, most of them purchased in early 2014 at Young Ones Records in Kutztown, Pennsylvania:

Heartbeat City—The Cars (released in March 1984)
Pyromania—Def Leppard (January 1983)
Robert Hazard—Robert Hazard (released sometime in 1982; records of this local Philadelphia release are quite hazy)
Quarterflash—Quarterflash (October 1981)
Moving Pictures—Rush (February 1981)
Tonight I'm Yours—Rod Stewart (November 1981)
The Dream of the Blue Turtles—Sting (July 1985)
Afterburner—ZZ Top (October 1985)

I'll freely admit that there was some "cheating" with our available music options. We also packed a Monster iCarPlay cassette adapter that allowed us to play music from our iPhones through that original (and pricey) Delco-GM/Bose car stereo, though this was at least from a large 1985 and older playlist. In the end, the two of us listened to far less music than I had expected to on this trip—I (seriously) wanted to hear if any parts were falling off the car.

Era-appropriate cassette tapes fill *Lauren*'s center console

Equipment and Tools in the Car

The two of us had these items packed in the back of *Lauren* when we began our trip:

Halon fire extinguisher
Combination battery charger and tire inflator
Mobil 1 synthetic oil (one quart) and oil rags
Two different but complementary multi-tools—a Leatherman Wave and a Victronix Swiss Army Knife CyberTool
An Eklind Ergo-Fold eight-size Torx wrench (C4 Corvettes have many Torx screws)
Ratchet wrench for dropping the small spare tire
First aid kit
Griot's Garage car cleaning supplies
And, watching over us, because it is always good to have capable and well-equipped professionals available: AAA Plus and Hagerty High-Octane.

Our Bests of the Trip

Best Diner: **Luxury Diner** in Cheyenne, Wyoming (Ivelis), **Original Mel's** in Placerville, California (John)
Best Fine Dining: **Elway's** in Denver (Ivelis and John)
Best Hotel: **Westin St. Francis** in San Francisco (Ivelis and John)
Best Day: North Platte, Nebraska to Rock Springs, Wyoming (Ivelis and John)
Best View: The Palisades in Green River, Wyoming (Ivelis), Bonneville Salt Flats (John)
Best Other Car: Pontiac Firebird Trans Am in Kansas (Ivelis and John)
Best City: Salt Lake City (Ivelis), Kansas City (John)
Best Town: Franklin Grove, Illinois (Ivelis and John)

When I'm compiling our bests for a trip, I write mine down first and then ask Ivelis for hers. Suffice to say that I was surprised at how much we agreed on about this 15-day jaunt.

Old Texaco in Potter, Nebraska

Things That I Know We Missed

I am confident that more knowledgeable or more experienced Lincoln Highway travelers would tell us that we missed many things—in part because of our notably quick pace compared to many who make this journey. We missed various cool sites around York, Pennsylvania because of the unexpected construction and the Rochelle Railroad Park in Illinois because I made the wrong turn in Aurora. Sadly, we also missed the Big Mac Museum in North Huntington, Pennsylvania.

Further west, I'll add all of Cedar Rapids, Iowa, the Union Pacific Railroad Museum in Council Bluffs, Iowa, and the Jelly Belly visitor's center in Fairfield, California to our misses. I also would have liked to have spent *more* time in Cheyenne, Wyoming, definitely visiting the Cheyenne Depot Museum.

Finally, the two of us also missed (because I couldn't find it even after much searching) the actual filming location of the Huey Lewis and the News "Heart and Soul" video in San Francisco.

ANNOTATED BIBLIOGRAPHY

Antonick, Mike. *Corvette Black Book 1953-2017*. Mount Vernon, OH: Michael Bruce, 2016.

The essential pocket Corvette reference (though you do need a *large* pocket), the *Corvette Black Book* will keep you from looking like a complete fool at almost any Corvette gathering, no matter what portions you are involved in of that widely ranging hobby. Mike Antonick revises and updates the *Black Book* every year (he's been at it since 1978), but mine (and it is far from my first) is now several years old—stained with dirt, brake fluid, and motor oil and full of notes and additional statistics. You should get the latest and greatest version.

Antonick, Mike. *Corvette Specs: 1984-1996 Models*. Minneapolis, MN: Motorbooks, 2002.

In this book, Antonick concentrates on only the C4 generation of Corvettes that were built from the 1984 to 1996 model years, exploring them in greater detail than I've seen anywhere else. Included are the most detailed production numbers currently available and the original Society of Automotive Engineers (SAE) specifications. I learned much about the specifics of my 1985 model while reading this book.

Butko, Brian. *Greetings from the Lincoln Highway: A Road Trip Celebration of America's First Coast-to-Coast Highway, Centennial Edition*. Mechanicsburg, PA: Stackpole, 2013.

Brian Butko has, I believe, written more books on the Lincoln Highway than anyone else—I count at least five. This *Centennial Edition* (second version) takes the reader from east to west. Butko doesn't cover every little town—rather, this book starts with a history of the Lincoln Highway and then gives an early traveler's sense of the experience. Out of print in the original paperback, but readily available as a well-designed Kindle edition.

Butko, Brian. *Lincoln Highway Companion*. Mechanicsburg, PA: Stackpole, 2009.

Brian Butko's small and wide (8.2 by 5.5 inches) *Lincoln Highway Companion* was our analog accompaniment to the TomTom software installed on our iPad mini—Ivelis had his book on hand right next to her for the entire trip as she toughed it out in *Lauren*'s passenger seat. Without it, our Lincoln Highway experience would not have been nearly as vibrant or as memorable—we would likely have missed the burgers at Kewpie, the Covered Wagon stand, the Luxury Diner, and the Lodgepole Opera House.

Still present, but status uncertain—the Thunderbird Lodge in downtown Laramie, Wyoming

A Complete Official Road Guide of the Lincoln Highway, Fifth Edition. Tucson, AZ: Patrice, 1993

In 1993, the Patrice Press published this fascinating facsimile reproduction of the voluminous (536 pages) fifth and final edition of the original Lincoln Highway Association's road guide, printed in 1924 and thus quite close to our chosen route. The reproduction paperback is currently out of print, but reasonably available in the used book market. I quote some still somewhat relevant advice from the *Official Road Guide* in this book.

Gutman, Richard. *American Diner Then and Now*. Baltimore, MD: The Johns Hopkins University Press, 2000.

American Diner Then and Now is perhaps the definitive book on the design and practice of the American diner. This book covers the history of diners from their humble beginnings in the late 1800s, their golden age in the 1920s and 1930s, their fading away under the assault of large fast food chains in the 1960s and 1970s, and their rediscovery in the 1980s and 1990s.

Lincoln Highway Association website, <www.lincolnhighwayassoc.org>

The relatively newly reconstituted Lincoln Highway Association's online presence includes much useful information, context, and advice, but the absolute star of their site is a fantastic, stunningly detailed, and extreme accurate Google Maps overlay of all the Lincoln Highway routes.

McLellan, David. *Corvette from the Inside: The Development History as told by Dave McLellan, Corvette's Chief Engineer 1975-1992*. Cambridge, MA: Bentley, 2002.

David McLellan, who was only the second chief Corvette engineer (after the legendary Zora Arkus-Duntov) since the introduction of the production car in 1953, gives much information and context on the engineering and design decisions that explain why the C4 Corvette ended up the way that it did, for better and for worse. With its strong emphasis on the many engineering considerations involved in creating four decades of Corvettes, *Corvette from the Inside* is a Corvette book like no other. McLellan, of course, is a hero to most C4 folks—we proudly display his signature on *Lauren*'s engine.

Ivelis made this picture happen—David McLellan and John posed in front of *Lauren* in July 2007

Wallis, Michael, and Williamson, Michael. *The Lincoln Highway*. New York, NY: Norton, 2007.

This dense and often gorgeous book (Williamson has deservedly won two Pulitzer prizes for photography) is positively not a travel guide but was one of our inspirational sources for this trip. Wallis also has written several books about Route 66 and is the voice of the Sheriff in all three of Pixar's *Cars* films.

Wilson, Jeff, and Rehberg, Randy, ed. *The Historical Guide to North American Railroads*, 3rd ed. Waukesha: Kalmbach, 2014.

There are so many great train books, but I find that this 300-odd page guide by the folks who publish the *Trains* and *Classic Trains* magazines is a helpful general reference that covers all North American railroad lines. Featuring many of both color and black and white photographs and at least one map per railroad listed.

Index

A
Abbottstown, PA 6
   Lincoln Speedway 6
Alfa Romeo Giulia Sprint coupe ix
American Graffiti film 46
Anson, "Cap" 20
Ardmore, PA x–xi, 5
   Frankel Chevrolet x
Argent, Lawrence 55
Arkus-Duntov, Zora 70
Asp, Lynn 18
Auburn, CA 49
   Black Bear Diner 49

B
Bedford, PA 8–9
   Dunkle's Gulf gas station 8
Bierce, Ambrose 14
Blair, John Insley 23
BMW R1100R motorcycle 48
Boeing VC-137C transport 66
Bonneville Salt Flats 38, 66
   Salt Flats Cafe 38
Boone, Colonel Nathan 21
Boone, Daniel 21
Bourbon, IN 15
Bowling Green, KY xi, xv
   Bowling Green Assembly Plant 9
   National Corvette Museum xi, 9
Bryn Mawr, PA 5, 64
Bucyrus, OH 12
Buick Electra 225 sedan 16
Bushnell, Cornelius Scranton 29

C
Car and Driver magazine ix–x, xiv
Carlisle, PA 64, 66
   Corvettes at Carlisle 64, 66
Cars films 70
Cavett, Dick 25
Chambersburg, PA 7
   30 West Family Restaurant 7
Chester, WV 11
   World's Largest Teapot 11
Chevrolet C/K pickup truck 6, 53
Chevrolet Corvette convertible xi, 46
Chevrolet Corvette Stingray coupe xv, 1, 64
Chevrolet Corvette Sting Ray coupe 50
Chevrolet Malibu Classic sedan 28
Cheyenne, WY 29–31
   Luxury Diner 29
City of Portland train 29
Clinton, IA 19
Cody, William "Buffalo Bill" 27
Cole, Ed xiii
Colo, IA 21
   Niland's Cafe 21
Columbus, NE 25
   Columbus Loup River Bridge 25
Columbus, OH 63
   Mitchell's Steakhouse 63
Contemporary Corvette viii, 5
Control Point 12
Convair B-58 Hustler strategic bomber 63
Copperfield, David 4
County Corvette viii
Cowher, Bill 11
Cussler, Clive 16

D
Dayton, OH 62–63, 66
   Wright-Patterson Air Force Base 62–63, 66
      National Museum of the United States Air Force 62–63, 66
Denison, IA 22
Denver, CO 54–55
   Colorado Convention Center 55
      Big Blue Bear statue 55
   Elway's Downtown steakhouse 54
   Westin Denver Downtown hotel 54
Dixon, IL 18, 77
Donner Pass 50
Dreiser, Theodore 14

E
East Liverpool, OH 11–12
Eisenhower, Dwight D. ix
Eisenhower-Johnson Memorial Tunnel 53
Ely, NV 39–43
   Hotel Nevada & Gambling Hall 41–42
      24-Hour Café 41–42
   Precision Auto Repair 41
Eureka, NV vii, 43
   Eureka Opera House vii, 43

Evanston, WY 36
  Jody's Diner 36

F
Fallon, NV 43–44
  Naval Strike and Air Warfare Center 44
Fisher, Carl Graham ix, 18, 61
Fonda, Henry 25
Ford F-series pickup truck 19
Fort Pitt Bridge 11
Franklin Grove, IL 17–18, 66
  Lincoln Way Cafe 18
Fremont, NE 24
  John C. Fremont City Park 24
Friedman, Milton 4
Fruita, CO 53
FWD truck 40

G
Gahman, Floyd 14
Gallup, George 22
General Electric diesel-electric locomotive 72

Union Pacific owned General Electric diesel-electric locomotive pushing a long freight train near Lowden, Iowa

Gettysburg, PA 6–7
Golden Gate Bridge 47
Grand Island, NE 25
Grand Junction, CO 53
Green River, WY 35
  Neldon's Custom Trim & Upholstery 34

H
Harah, Bob 10
Harlem Globetrotters 17
Hetzel, Bill 50–51

Higgins, Andrew Jackson 25
Hill, David xvi
Hitchcock, Alfred 2
Huston, John 44
Hutton, Lauren xii

I
"Ideal Section" 14, 18–19
Imperial, PA 11
  Kings Family Restaurant 11
Indianapolis, IN 59–61
  Indianapolis Power & Light Company building 60
  Ruth's Chris Steak House 60
  Soldiers and Sailors monument 60

J
Jaguar E-Type convertible 13
Jarrett, Dale 62
Jeep Grand Wagoneer SUV 36
Jefferson, IA 21
Jennings Randolph Bridge 11
Jordan, Ned 31
Jordan Playboy roadster 31–32

K
Kansas City, MO 56–58
  Fiorella's Jack Stack Barbecue 57
  Liberty Memorial 56
  Union Station 57
  Western Auto Building 57–58
  Westin Crown Center hotel 56–58
Kearney, NE 25
  Covered Wagon 26
Koontz, Dean 8
Kutztown, PA xvii, 67
  Young Ones Records xvii, 67
Kyburz, CA 45

L
Lages Station, NV 39, 76
  Stage Stop Bar-Cafe 39, 76
Lancaster, PA 6, 66
La Ramée, Jacques 31
Laramie, WY 31, 69
  Thunderbird Lodge 31, 69
Lawrenceville, NJ 4–5
  Michael's Family Restaurant & Diner 4
LeMond, Greg 44
Lewis, Huey 48, 68

Lexington, NE 26
  Hollingsworth Motel 26
Life magazine 42
Ligonier, Field Marshal John 9
Lima, OH 13
  Kewpee fast food restaurant 13
Lincoln Highway Association xviii, 14, 17–18, 66
Lincoln Tunnel 1, 4
Lisbon, OH 12
Lodgepole, NE 28
  Lodgepole Opera House 28–29
Lovelock, NV 51
Lowden, IA 72
Lower Trenton Bridge 5
LTV A-7 Corsair II attack aircraft 44

M
M1 Abrams main battle tank 23
Marshalltown, IA 20–22
Matteson, IL 16, 65
  Lincoln Mall 16, 65
McClead, Jordan 14, 48
McLellan, David 52, 70
Medicine Bow, WY 34
  Virginian Hotel 34
Metaphor: The Tree of Utah sculpture 37
Metroliner trains 4
Michael Mina's Bourbon Steak restaurant 66
Minerva, OH 12
Missouri Valley, IA 22
Momen, Karl 37
Monitor ironclad warship 29
Morton salt plant 37
Motor Trend magazine x
Mulhern, Lt. Col. John ix, x

N
New York Central railroad 4
New York, NY ix, 1–4, 65
  Chrysler Building 2
  King Features Syndicate 2
  Palm restaurant 65
  The Capital Grille restaurant 2
  The Palm restaurant 2
  Times Square ix, 1, 3–4
  United Nations 2
  Waldorf Astoria hotel 1–3
    Peacock Alley Bar & Lounge 2
Nicks, Stevie viii
Nissan Maxima sedan x

North by Northwest film 2
North Platte, NE 26–27
  Fort Cody Trading Post 26

O
Ogallala, NE 27
  Lamp Stand coffee shop 27
Overland Limited train 31

P
Palmer, Jerry 66
Pennsylvania Railroad 5, 14
Philadelphia, PA 5
Pittsburgh, PA 5, 9–12
  Alcoa building 10
  Omni William Penn hotel 9–10
    The Tap Room bar 10
    The Terrace Room restaurant 10
Placerville, CA 46
  Original Mel's 46
Pontiac Firebird Trans Am coupe 56
Pony Express 43
Porsche Cayenne SUV 35
Porter, John xvii
Portland, OR xvi
  Fred Bauer Chevrolet xvi
Potter, NE 29, 68

Q
Queneau, Bernie 66

R
Rahway, NJ 4
Ram pickup truck 45
Reagan, Ronald 18
Reno, NV 50–51
Republic F-105 Thunderchief fighter-bomber 77
Reynolds, Burt 56
Ringwald, Molly 49
Rock Springs, WY 34
Ronks, PA 6
  Dutch Haven store 6
  Route 30 Diner 6
Route 66 xvii, 16

S
Salem, OR xii
  Delon BMW xii
Salt Lake City, UT 36–37
  Mormon Tabernacle 36

San Francisco, CA ix, 47–49, 68
  1906 San Francisco earthquake 48
  Lincoln Park ix, 47
    Legion of Honour 48
  Westin St. Francis hotel 48–49
    Michael Mina's Bourbon Steak restaurant 48
Saratoga Auto Museum xv
Schellsburg, PA 8–9
  Bison Corral 8
  Grand View Hotel 8–9
Schuyler, NE 24
Scranton, Joseph H. 22
"Seedling Miles" 14, 17–18, 25
Shabbona, IL 17
Shelton, NE 25
  Lincoln Highway Visitor's Center 25
Smokey and the Bandit film 56
Speedway, IN 61–62, 74
  Indianapolis Motor Speedway 61–62, 74

Stateline, NV 44–46
  Harveys Casino 45
    Sage Room Steak House 45
  Lakeside Inn and Casino 44–45
Sterling, IL 18
Sugar Grove, IL 17

T
Tama, IA 20
  Lincoln Highway bridge 20
The Misfits film 44
The Saturday Evening Post magazine 31–32
The Wall Street Journal newspaper x
Trenton, NJ 5

U
Union Pacific trains 23–24, 26, 29, 31, 72

V
Vandalia, IL 59
  Sonic drive-in restaurant 58–59
Villanova, PA 6
Volkswagen Vanagon Westfalia van 18

W
Ward's Quarterly magazine 6
Warsaw, IN 14–15
Washington, DC 62
  Smithsonian Air & Space Museum 62
Wayne, "Mad" Anthony 6
Weehawken, NJ 1, 4
  The Helix 1
West Valley City, UT 51
  TGI Fridays restaurant 51
West Wendover, NV 38–39
Wheldon, Dan 61

X

Y

Z

Looking up at the famous "pagoda" at the Indianapolis Motor Speedway in Speedway, Indiana

CREDITS

All maps copyright © 2018 Map Resources, modified by John Mulhern III

All other images (80) copyright © 2018 Ivelis Mulhern *unless* otherwise listed below

Front and back cover, pages i, x (automobile magazines and model), xii, xiii (engine), xiv, xv, 1 (starting mileage), 2 (Manhattan and Chrysler Building), 4 (*Lauren* in Times Square), 7 (fuel reserve and *Lauren* outside restaurant), 8 (mural), 10, 11 (former Alcoa building), 12 (*Lauren* behind gas pumps), 13 (Kewpee), 14 (texts), 15 (Lincoln Highway sign), 17, 20 (Tama bridge), 24, 27 (*Lauren* in front of gas station), 28, 30, 33, 34 (*Lauren* at Neldon's Custom Trim), 36, 40 (offending part), 41 (Precision Auto Repair sign), 45 (*Lauren* with truck), 46 (*Lauren* with mid-year), 47 (mileage and Jordan), 48 (view of Union Square), 52 (helicopter), 53 (truck framing *Lauren*), 54 (shrimp and seasoning), 55, 57, 59 (*Lauren* at a Sonic), 60, 61 (Ivelis in pressroom), 62 (Ivelis kisses bricks and wind tunnel), 63 (B58 and fire house), 64 (final mileage and bugs on front bumper), 65, 66 (old Goodyear dealer), 67, 74, 75, and all route markers copyright © 2018 John Mulhern III

Photo on page ix courtesy of Margaret Antkowiak

Classified advertisement from the Philadelphia Inquirer on page x courtesy of newspapers.com

50th Anniversary Corvette Caravan logo on page xi © 2003 National Corvette Museum

Photo of *Lauren* in Wildwood on page xiii courtesy of Adam Wald

DieHard image on page xvi courtesy of Sears

TireRack logo on page xvi courtesy of TireRack

Young Ones Records logo on page xvii courtesy of Young Ones Records

Waldorf Astoria New York logo on page 1 copyright © 2018 Hilton Worldwide

Commemorative plaque in Franklin Grove, Illinois

Photo of Waldorf Astoria motor lobby on page 2 copyright © 2018 Hilton Worldwide

Photo of Omni William Penn on page 9 copyright © 2018 Omni Hotels

Photo of World's Largest Teapot on page 11 courtesy of Wikipedia contributor Kurtsampsel

The Union Pacific logo on page 22 is the registered mark of Union Pacific Railroad, used with permission

Photo of "seedling mile" on page 25 courtesy of the National Park Service

Quote passage on page 31 from page 41 of *A Complete Official Road Guide of the Lincoln Highway, Fifth Edition.* Tucson, AZ: Patrice, 1993

Official Highway 50 Survival Guide cover on page 42 courtesy of the State of Nevada

Photo of F-5 Tiger II on page 44 courtesy of the U.S. Navy, taken by Mass Communication Specialist 1st Class Joseph R. Vincent

Photo of Sony RX100 on page 45 courtesy of Sony

Picture of Lincoln Highway marker on page 48 courtesy of Flickr contributor Rob Cordor

75

Photo of *Lauren* on page 50 courtesy of Bill Hetzel

Elway's Downtown logo on page 54 courtesy of Elway's

Fiorella's Jack Stack Barbecue logo on page 58 courtesy of Jack Stack Barbecue

Aerial photo of the National Museum of the United States Air Force on page 76 courtesy of the U.S. Air Force, taken by Ben Strasser.

Passing the remains of the Stage Stop Bar-Cafe at the intersection of Route 93A and US Route 93 in the ghost town of Lages Station, Nevada

About the Author

After serving as an avionics technician in the U.S. Navy, John Mulhern III attended Drexel University, receiving a BS in Information Systems with concentrations in artificial intelligence, database development, and human interface design.

John has worked at the University of Pennsylvania for over 25 years. He is currently Principal Technology Advisor, a role in which he focuses on the future computing needs of everyone from first-year students to emeritus faculty members.

John has published two books previously under the J3Studio Press imprint. The first was *A 21st Century Road Trip*, which was released in 2006 and chronicles a 2005 trip on Route 66 and the Pacific Coast Highway in a Corvette convertible. The second was *Slightly Slower 66*, which was released in 2016 and describes a 2015 trip along Route 66 in a Corvette coupe. John writes a fairly active blog on *all* vehicles of the eighties, which can be found at eightiescars.com

John resides in Bryn Mawr, Pennsylvania with his lovely wife Ivelis, and his beloved Corvettes: *Lauren*, *Grace*, and *Louis*.

About the Principal Photographer

Ivelis Mulhern attended Drexel University, receiving a BS in Business Administration with concentrations in accounting and finance. While at Drexel, she sang mezzo-soprano with multiple groups and played the female lead in *Man of La Mancha* during her senior year.

Ivelis is currently a Certified Financial Planner™ Practioner with Ameriprise Financial Services, Inc and has been with Ameriprise (and its predecessor American Express Financial Advisors) since 1996. She resides in Bryn Mawr, Pennsylvania with her husband John, with whom she has been married for over 20 years.

Ivelis daily drives a *much* more modern Corvette than *Lauren*: *Louis*, a black 2012 Centennial Edition Chevrolet Corvette coupe with 436 horsepower, a trick exhaust, racing stripes, and a little bit of a mean streak. You can read much more about *Louis* in *Slightly Slower 66* (J3Studio Press, 2016)

Republic F-105 Thunderchief fighter-bomber on display in Dixon, Illinois

www.ingramcontent.com/pod-product-compliance
Lightning Source LLC
Chambersburg PA
CBHW041432010526
44118CB00002B/57